Lancaste

R. Follows.

Tin-glazed Earthenware

Tin-glazed Earthenware

From Maiolica, Faience and Delftware
to the contemporary

Daphne Carnegy

A & C Black · London
Chilton Book Company · Radnor, Pennsylvania

First published in Great Britain 1993
A & C Black (Publishers) Limited
35 Bedford Row, London WC1R 4JH

ISBN 0-7136-3718-8

Copyright © 1993 by Daphne Carnegy

A CIP catalogue record for this book is available from
the British Library

First published in USA by Chilton Book Company, Radnor,
Pennsylvania 19089

ISBN 0-8019-8487-4

Jacket illustrations
front: dish by Author, photograph by Stephen Brayne
back: detail of dish by Author

Frontispiece:
Daphne Carnegy, storage jars, large one ht 30 cm, 1986.
Photograph by Tim Hill.

Designed by Janet Watson

Typeset by Florencetype Ltd, Kewstoke, Avon
Printed and bound in Great Britain by
Butler and Tanner Ltd, Frome and London

Contents

Acknowledgements   6
Introduction   7

SECTION I: HISTORICAL SURVEY   11
  Early Tin Glaze: From Islamic to Hispano-Moresque   12
  Italian Maiolica   24
  French Faience   37
  The Netherlands – Delftware   44
  English Delftware   51
  Cross-Fertilisations   60
  The Artist's Medium   65

SECTION II: MATERIALS AND TECHNIQUES   75
  The Legacy of Piccolpasso   76

Materials and Kilns   77
  Clays   77
  Glazes   78
  Glaze Composition Today   79
  Fluxes   79
  Felspars and Secondary Fluxes   80
  Opacifiers   80
  Pigments   81
  Reduced-Pigment Lustres   86
  Kilns   88

Techniques   90
  Preparation of the Glaze   90
  Preparation of Pots for Glazing   90
  Glazing   90
  Sintering   91
  Brushes and Brushwork   92
  Painting Mediums   93
  The Author's Painting Technique   93
  Other Methods of Decoration   95
  Firing   97
  Troubleshooting – Common problems in   97
    tin-glazed earthenware
  Toxicity   98

SECTION III: CONTEMPORARY PERSPECTIVES   101

  Part 1:   Individual Approaches
              Tin-glazed Earthenware in the Studio Context   102

  Part 2:   Tradition and Innovation
              Some Aspects of Workshop and Factory Production   159

  Tables: Composition of Ferro leadless frits and Potterycrafts frits 168
  Table: Orton pyrometic cones   169
  List of suppliers   170
  List of museums   171
  Bibliography   172
  Map showing main historical centres of manufacture of
    tin-glazed earthenware in Europe   174
  Index   175

Acknowledgements

Many people have helped to make this book possible – makers and non-makers alike – by giving so generously of time, information, material, and often hospitality as well. I would particularly like to thank William Newland, for stimulating discussions and provision of archive material; Alan Caiger-Smith, whose knowledge has been such a cornerstone and whose publications I have drawn on heavily; Walter Ostrom and Andrea Gill for putting me in touch with new dimensions in contemporary maiolica and for their insightful contributions; Kenneth and Ann Clark for interesting recollections. Special thanks are due to John Houston for his encouragement and constructive criticism; to David Gaimster and Dora Thornton at the British Museum and Miss Julia Poole at the Fitzwilliam Museum, for giving their valuable time and knowledge; to Timothy Wilson and Dr James Allan at the Ashmolean Museum for very kindly reading through the text of the historical section and making helpful comments; to all museum staff who have generously made materials available; to Marc Camille Chaimowicz for opening up new vistas; to Stephen Brayne and Douglas Cape for photography; to Ubaldo Grazia and Pieter Jan Tichelaar for their cooperation; to Dr Philip Jackson at CERAM Research for providing the latest information on lead and cadmium release; to Victor Bryant for checking the technical text; to Anne Barlow and Margaret Harrison for access to their Quimper collections; to Helen Ellis for providing all the material on her cousin, Margrit Linck; also to Anthony Ray, Murray Fieldhouse, Marie Miler, Carew Treffgarne, Richard Zakin, Dominik Pferlmutter, Doris Kuyken-Schneider, Allard Hidding, François Bernard, Faienceries H. B. Henriot, Dr Ottfried Schroeder, Karen Tischendorf; to all those who sent material which unfortunately, for reasons of space, it has not been possible to include; to all those who have responded to impromptu telephone queries; to my editor Linda Lambert for her assistance, sympathy and extreme patience; and last but not least to Rick for more than his fair share of entertaining our lively two-year-old, Theo.

Introduction

What is tin-glazed earthenware? For many people it is synonymous with 'maiolica', with the glaze as a ground for painting on – like a painter's canvas. Although maiolica is an important aspect of tin-glazed earthenware, it is not the complete story. Tin glaze is not so much a technique – a tin glaze is after all merely one which is rendered opaque and white by the addition of tin oxide. As such it is more of a medium which, through the centuries, has adapted itself to a great diversity of expressive functions. There have been numerous examples of tin glaze employed for its own surface qualities, unpainted, as a complement to formal, plastic concerns, or in combination with other decorative techniques. The term 'tin-glazed earthenware' therefore refers, in this book, to the medium as a whole. As to the term 'maiolica', this is used historically, in the context of the Italian Renaissance (in which case it is referred to as 'Italian maiolica'). It is also used as a generic term for painted tin glaze, i.e. when the pigments are painted on to the freshly applied glaze and become fused into the glaze in the subsequent firing. The correct technical term for the process is 'in-glaze' painting. 'Maiolica' is not to be confused with 'Majolica', which can only legitimately be used to describe the range of earthenware developed by Mintons in the 1840s, initially inspired by but technically and stylistically unrelated to Italian maiolica. Other terms for tin-glazed earthenware, such as the French 'faience' and Dutch and English 'delftware' are clarified at their appropriate historic moments.

For virtually three centuries, from the early Renaissance to the advent of Wedgwood, tin-glazed earthenware dominated the pottery market in Europe. That in itself is an extraordinary phenomenon. Its origins can be traced back through Moorish Spain to 9th century Islam. In the guises of maiolica, faience and delftware, it lent itself to the expression of a succession of tastes and fashions which virtually simultaneously swept through the Western world and were manifest in every area of the fine and applied arts. The crude apothecary shapes and Gothic ornament of the end of the 15th century gave way to the purely decorative pot, whose surface as a canvas played host to complex virtuoso performances of High Renaissance narrative painting. The 17th century ushered in cool classicism, fanciful chinoiserie, generous Baroque, and the debut of tin-glazed earthenware as grand and fashionable tableware. The crisp asymmetry, floral sprays, naturalism and rose-madder hues of Rococo dominated the 18th century. In each country, there were cultural modulations and shifts of emphasis, but essentially the conventions were prescribed. Today we respond very differently to these historical models. I have tried to present each style within the framework of the particular place and time, as well as occasionally putting forward a contemporary or personal aesthetic viewpoint.

The aesthetic appeal of tin-glazed earthenware was due to two main factors: the whiteness of the glaze and its potential for colour. The white glaze, like that of its inspiration, Chinese porcelain, suggested notions of purity, refinement, status and expense. Its ability to maximise colour in a luminous fusion of glaze and pigment presented a marked contrast to the earthy utilitarian medieval pottery and took ceramics into the realm of the exotic, of 'treasure'.[1] The white glaze provided an open invitation for pattern and imagery, for the figurative and the narrative. The very separateness of the thick glaze surface from the underlying body predisposed a dominant concern with surface. With division of labour and the influence of the fine arts, Italian maiolica crystallised a hierarchical distinction between content (the painting) and form (the blank), which was to remain a largely inherent characteristic of the tin-glaze tradition. Maiolica became inseparable from its pictorial role; with ornament borrowed from paintings, engravings and prints it became the broadcaster of art to a very wide market.

Whilst writing, I became increasingly aware of the phenomenon of imitation as a fundamental aspect of the tradition.[2] Chinese porcelain was the most persistent and recurrent source of imitation, initially for the invention of the tin glaze itself, and subsequently for ornament, shapes and colour groupings. Painting too was a constant source of reference; forms and decorative motifs were also adopted from other applied arts, notably metalwork and textiles. Within the discipline of tin glaze itself, hybrids and cross-pollinations abound; for example, the bizarre motifs of ancient Roman 'grotto-paintings', popularised by Raphael's decoration of the Vatican Loggias, became the 'grotesques' of High Renaissance maiolica ornament. They were to appear again in the Netherlands, England, Spain and France, modified by local taste. Venetian fruit designs filtered through to early Netherlandish tiles and English chargers. In France, Baroque paintings in Italianate colours adorned Chinese baluster shapes. In the Netherlands, humble porringers depicted pious Flemish madonnas surrounded by oriental patterns.

It is perhaps this readiness of tin glaze to mimic, absorb and present such a variety of personas, which has, in the recent past, most handicapped its reputation. Its emphasis on surface, seen as frivolous and fickle, embodies the very antithesis of such Modernist principles as 'truth to materials', 'form follows function' and a rejection of historicism. Michael Cardew once described maiolica as distorting the majesty of form. It became linked to a second-hand aesthetic: Bernard Leach writing in 1940[3] described Italian maiolica as 'generally weak, ornate and closely allied to third-rate Renaissance painting'. He was slightly more complimentary about Dutch delftware, but only in reference to its near-perfect Chinese imitations.

Since the demise of tin glaze as a form of pottery available, in high art or in folk art, to a whole cross-section of society, there have only been occasional excursions into the medium by artists and applied-art groups. In England, tin glaze enjoyed an explosive postwar revival; William Newland was one of its founder members. Initially inspired by the ceramics of Picasso, it brought a refreshing, decorative *joie-de-vivre* after a grim, colourless period, but in the 1960s, domestic stoneware glazed in celadons and tenmokus was again in the ascendancy and dominated the market until, in the mid-1970s, Alison Britton, Jacqueline Poncelet and Elizabeth Fritsch set the trend for handbuilt, contemplative, abstract vessels.

The long duration and complex nature of the tin-glaze tradition has left a weighty aesthetic heritage which cannot be ignored. In looking at contemporary tin-glaze practitioners, I have tried to elucidate their diverse attitudes to the tradition and how they work from it, with it or against it, or indeed whether they refer to it at all. It is no accident that tin glaze is being brought into quite extensive use again now. In a spirit of Post-modernist eclecticism, many artists are self-consciously, and ambiguously, making use of the tradition. Alison Britton[4] has described her approach (and that of her contemporaries) as both needing and recognising tradition but 'inventing freely on top of it'. It is interesting that this self-conscious way of working described by Britton, seems to apply particularly to the North American maiolica makers. Working in a complex, sophisticated way, they are far removed from domestic production potters, and yet the vessel is still their concern. Italian maiolica provides them with a perfect 'pedigree of the useless pot'[5]. Maybe their real distance from historical tradition gives these makers freedom to refer to it in such a bold and explicit way. Andrea Gill, Walter Ostrom, Terry Siebert, Bruce Cochrane and Ian Symons all cultivate a sense of continuity and make both direct and extended reference to traditional vocabulary of ceramic form and ornament, but it is used in such a way as to contain an element of irony; the maker is both participant and observer. Tradition is quoted, reworked to suit new purposes. These are the modern hybrid pots. Forms are often complex; in the case of Gill, handbuilt and multifaceted; with Ostrom and Cochrane, shapes are thrown, altered, modelled, pierced and assembled to create particular environments for particular imagery or surfaces. Gill has likened tin glaze to a loose skin which provides a shaped canvas for further exploration, and all her work is about the relationship of form to surface content. Illusionism is also an important element of the new decorative pot. Pots are painted to look like other things; colour and pattern are employed as modulators of perception. The work of Richard and Carol Selfridge for example makes use of *trompe l'oeil* and playful interaction between form and image. Agalis Manessi, in a gentle, understated way, is also concerned with such issues. She also makes frequent reference to the still life, aware that her pots when finished will form part of a larger domestic still life themselves.

Whilst being acutely aware of tradition, Alan Caiger-Smith does not manipulate it or make observations about it. There is no direct quotation. The references, in Caiger-Smith's case mostly Islamic and Hispano-Moresque, are experienced as an underlying nourishing influence, absorbed and filtered through passion into the maker's aesthetic. Through his in-glaze and reduced-pigment lustre painting, Caiger-Smith creates an abstract calligraphic dance which draws the eye across the contours of the pot. Alan Peascod also works in lustres on tin glaze, alongside his current interest in dry surfaces. He too has made informed use of the Islamic tradition to create his own individual language.

A decorative pot can often be defined by its external references – George Woodman wrote: 'The desire of the object to reach out and connect with many other kinds of things and situations is characteristic of the decorative'[6] – and by its function in the decoration of a specific context. It is 'embellished to decorate something else'.[7] A distinction can be made between the outward-looking 'decorative' pot and the 'painted' pot which has more parallels with serious works of art and where the pot is a canvas to be painted for its own sake. The references might be personal-symbolic, mythological, narrative, figurative or purely abstract. Deirdre Daw, Jane Gustin and Jitka Palmer all use maiolica in this painterly way. More sculptural in concept, further removed from the everyday vessel, but definitely 'painted' are the works of Gilbert Portanier and Matthias Ostermann. Outside of either the decorative or the painted category and in complete contrast, Margrit Linck's work is not concerned with either quotation or content, only with structure. Its origins are primitive, organic, the references figurative but oblique. Here, the tin glaze is a means to achieving a particular quality of surface; its unadorned whiteness speaks only of the form. In the realm of domestic pottery, there is a diversity of statements, from the magnificent to the casual, from the minimalist to the chintzy.

Deirdre Daw, teapot, cups and saucers, 'Christopher Columbus discovers indigenous vegetables' from 'Christopher Columbus invades America' series, teapot ht 41 cm, 1991. Double-walled, carved.

Whatever the nature of the work, utilitarian, decorative, sculptural or architectural, I have tried throughout the individual case studies not only to define the maker's stance *viv-à-vis* tradition but also to establish his/her particular attraction to the medium of tin glaze and to convey design and practice criteria. Tiles are not the main concern of this book – they require a complete one to themselves – but I have covered salient historical aspects as well as showing contemporary examples. The same goes for lustreware. The section on Materials and Techniques is intended both as a theoretical and empirical reference for tin-glaze practitioners and as an explanatory prelude to the individual case studies where practice is discussed in some detail.

Most of the contemporary examples of studio-produced tin-glazed earthenware come from the USA, Canada, England and Australia. Apart from England, none of these countries has any history of tin glaze, and even the English tradition was not as long-lived as those of its Continental counterparts. In those countries which had the strongest tin-glaze traditions, I have been least successful in locating contemporary examples of studio work in the medium. Maybe the weight of tradition is so great that satisfactory contemporary expressions have not yet been found. Studio pottery in Italy and Holland, for example, seems to be more design-orientated. In France, potters are attracted to the more earthy mediums of stoneware and slipware. The dearth of individual-made tin glaze in certain countries led me to look at the production of tin glaze on a larger scale – in the factory or the family workshop. In many cases, tradition is adhered to unquestioningly; but I also found evidence of new attitudes to design and enterprising investment in the contemporary.

Finally a word about the technical parameters of this book. Although the title refers to tin-glazed earthenware, I have not been purist in my search for contemporary idioms. Of course, there are tin-glaze potters who still believe in and stick to traditional methods. However, just as, for reasons of health and safety, many glazes are now leadless, so expensive tin oxide is nowadays often replaced, either totally or in part by the cheaper zirconium silicate, an equally efficient opacifier. A zirconium-opacified glaze does have a few differing properties, but essentially it serves the same purposes as a tin-opacified glaze and as such it deserves to be included. The medium has had to move with the times.

Notes

[1] A term used by Philip Rawson in his book, *Ceramics*, London (Oxford University Press, 1971)

[2] This is a subject explored in broader context by Anne Lajoix in her article 'Céramique et mise en abîme de l'imitation', *Caravelles 2*, catalogue of the 2e Quadriennale Internationale de Design, Lyon, 1991

[3] In *A Potter's Book*, London (Faber and Faber, 1940)

[4] In her article, 'Sèvres with Krazy Kat', *Crafts Magazine*, no. 61, 1983

[5] Alison Britton on Italian maiolica in *Crafts Magazine*, no. 87, 1987

[6] George Woodman in his article, 'Ceramic Decoration and the Concept of Ceramics as a Decorative Art', *American Ceramics*, vol. I, no. 1, Winter 1982. His definitions of decorated, decorative and painted pots have informed and underpinned many observations made during the course of this book.

[7] Woodman ibid.

Detail of jug, Faenza, late 15th or early 16th century. Museó del Vino, Torgiano, Lungarotti Foundation

SECTION I
Historical Survey

Early Tin Glaze

From Islamic to Hispano-Moresque

Early Islamic

It is extraordinary to think that the whole decorative tradition of tin-glazed earthenware which dominated European ceramics from the early 1500s until the advent of Wedgwood had its foundation in 9th century Iraq, in the form of an adventurous imitation of Chinese porcelain, and owes its exuberant character to the innate Islamic love of colour and pattern. The spread and development of the technique from its inception in Iraq was inextricably linked to the rapid growth of Islam, which, within little more than a century, was to become greater in size than even the Roman Empire, extending right across North Africa and up into Spain.

Although the cultural roots of Islam were widespread – Roman, Greek, Byzantine, Egyptian, Persian and Turkic influences all played their part – Islamic art quite quickly developed a very strong identity of its own. Craftsmen came from all over the empire to work at the Caliphs' court, be it Baghdad, Cairo or Cordoba, and when one dynasty fell, another rose and the craftsmen moved on to the new centre of artistic activity. There were therefore noticeable similarities of style throughout the Islamic countries at any given time.

The first experiments in tin glaze were carried out under the patronage of the Abbasid caliphate. These were in emulation of the much admired and expensive Chinese T'ang porcelain, which was imported to Iraq mainly by sea, via the Indian Ocean and the Persian Gulf. These fine wares had been a revelation to the Arab craftsmen, opening their eyes to the aesthetic potential of pottery. A demand began to grow from the court and the ruling classes for fine and sophisticated pottery which the craftsmen were quick to exploit. New workshops were established under the patronage of the court. Not having access to high-firing porcelain-type clays, the nearest the craftsmen could get to the effect of white porcelain was to opacify their already existing, low-temperature clear alkaline glazes with tin oxide, thus producing a mattish, thick white glaze to cover up the buff-coloured earthenware body. Iraq had no tin of its own and this material was imported from Malaysia and Burma – a reflection of the wide trade links of early Islam.[1]

Imitation however very quickly gave way to native creative energy; the Islamic potters couldn't resist decorating the plain white surface and thus began to create their own distinctive decorative idiom, which could hardly be further removed from the restrained Chinese originals (T'ang porcelain had minimal decoration – usually in the form of low-relief carving – and certainly no coloured brushwork). These simple early designs show a strong sense of composition; the motifs were often based on stylised floral patterns (e.g. the palmette and the arabesque), Kufic inscriptions or geometric devices. Ornament also came from metalwork and carved wood. A natural sensibility to the varying qualities of brushwork is evident in the manner of painting, sometimes fine and graphic, sometimes bold and painterly (see photograph on p. 13). Some designs incorporated attempts to imitate the T'ang runny lead-glazed ware by the splashing on of copper oxide (see photograph on p.14). The shapes of the small bowls with flared rims and shallow footrings derive from Chinese examples, whilst the flat-rimmed plates are probably based on metalware forms.

The main oxide used for decorating was cobalt. This is the first known use of this colourant in pottery and the direct source of the Chinese adoption of the blue and white colour scheme[2] which in its turn came to be imitated with such fervour in the Western tin-glaze tradition. The oxides, strong enough to penetrate the opaque glaze, were at this stage applied as underglaze pigments. As the technique of tin glaze spread to Syria and Egypt, the palette changed from the predominant cobalt blue to manganese browns and copper greens.

Flat dish, diam. 30 cm, Iraq 9th century.
Decorated with cobalt blue on white tin glaze. Here the style of painting is bolder and more painterly than the dish in the photograph on p. 14 and the design itself is quite unusual for the period. This colour combination was much admired by the Chinese and was the inspiration for their own, and in its turn much imitated, blue and white decoration.
Ashmolean Museum, Oxford

Lustre painting on tin glaze

Concurrent with the development of simple oxide decoration was the application of reduced-pigment lustres, also on tin glaze. This technique had its origin in pre-Islamic Egypt, where copper and silver stains were used on glass, which was much admired in Mesopotamia. It was quickly adapted to the decoration of pottery. There is no record of the exact techniques employed at the time, but it is likely that compounds of silver and copper were used to produce a variety of lustre effects, from yellow, amber and orange to greens, browns and rich coppery reds. The compounds were probably ground with sulphur, dissolved in vinegar or grape juice and mixed with red or yellow ochre to a paintable consistency.

Application was carried out on to the already fired glaze surface. The ware was then refired in a smokey, reduction atmosphere to a temperature at which the underlying glaze will just soften (a low red heat). On removal from the kiln, the unfused ochre was gently rubbed away. If all went well, the pigments, starved of oxygen in the firing, would have been reduced to a film of lustrous metal on the surface of the pot. It is an extremely hazardous technique, the outcome being highly sensitive to variations and irregularities of application or firing.

The technique of lustreware spread throughout Islam and up into Spain, where it reached a zenith in Hispano-Moresque ware. Apart from the splendid examples of Deruta and Gubbio, lustres were not used again in Europe until the 19th-century revival of interest in medieval techniques.

Most of the examples of the earliest Abbasid lustreware are in the form of small bowls or shallow, flat-rimmed plates but sturdy jars and tiles were also made. At first the lustre work was polychrome, probably a result of experimentation with varying thicknesses of compounds.[3] Later, when more skill and knowledge and control had been acquired through practice of the technique, it became less risky to use just one colour lustre, and the use of polychrome lustres died out. The designs of the lustreware are, apart from some similarity of the odd motif and border, surprisingly different from those of the oxide in-glaze decorated ware. The polychrome lustred pots are wild and busy, decorated all over with juxtaposed patterns of circles, squares, dots, chevrons, herringbones, cross-hatching, half-palmettes, within a loose floral or geometric composition. There is one example of a bird design (in the Ashmolean Museum) which is quite different from the others and would appear to be a prototype of designs to come. These new dramatic designs feature a prominent single subject – a stylised bird, animal, human figure, even a pot (these must

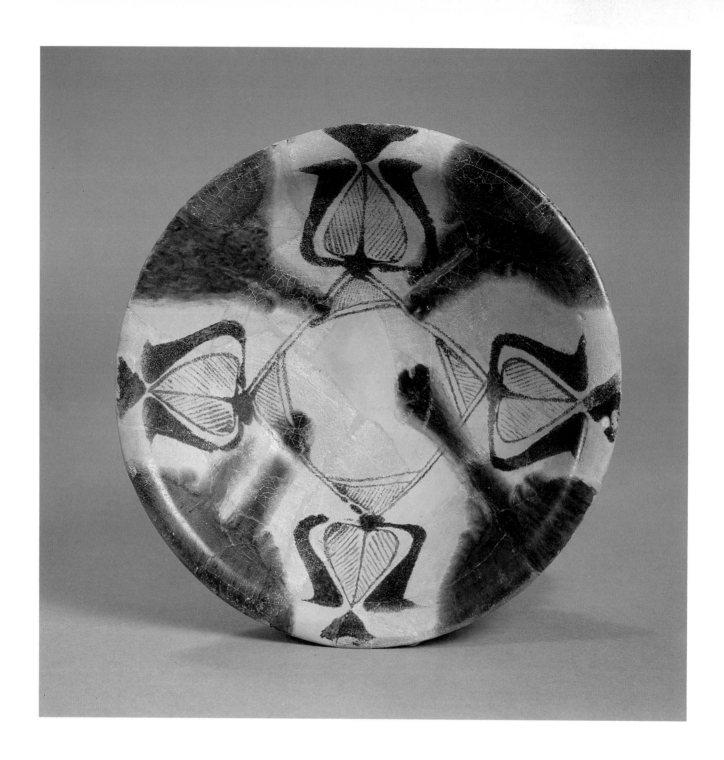

Bowl, diam. 20.2 cm, ht 6 cm, Iraq 9th century
Painting in cobalt with splashes of copper on tin glaze.
This design shows the Islamic love of geometric pattern
and a natural tendency to formalise – the four motifs are
palmettes which derive from a stylised flower pattern.
The copper splashes are an attempt to imitate T'ang runny
lead-glazed ware.
Ashmolean Museum, Oxford

surely be the earliest examples of the 'pot on a
pot' theme) – which fills a large proportion of the
painted area. This is thrown into relief by a
contour line which both creates an outer definition of the main subject and contains an all
over background patterning (see photograph on
p. 15). This device, known as the 'contour panel'
was popular in Islamic art and continued to be
used right through to Hispano-Moresque and
Italian wares.

Small bowl with lustre-painted decoration on tin glaze, diam. 11.9 cm, ht 2.7 cm, Iraq 10th century.
The contour panel framing the central subject (an ibex) and the half-moon border are typical early Islamic design conventions. A strong sense of composition and feeling for the form is evident.
Keir Collection (courtesy of Edmund de Unger)

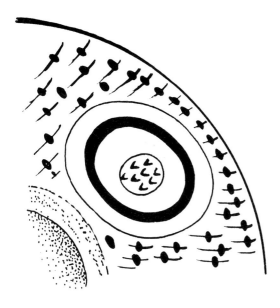

The underside is freely painted with circles, dashes and blobs. The refreshing loosening-up on the backs of bowls and dishes is characteristic of much Islamic pottery and reaches its zenith with Hispano-Moresque ware.
Keir Collection (courtesy of Edmund de Unger)

Fatimid lustreware of Egypt

As production of tin-glazed lustreware went into decline in Mesopotamia, so there arose, in the 10th century, a new school of lustre painting in Egypt under the patronage of the Fatimid Caliphate court in Cairo. Many of the most talented potters from Baghdad migrated to the new centre of activity; the schism with Baghdad fuelled artistic energies and gave a fresh impetus to the production of pottery.

The shapes are, again, simple bowls, some with convex, some with straight sides, but there are also some full-bellied jars with short necks.

Large jar with 'blind' handles, ht 35.5 cm, lustre on tin glaze. Egypt, Fatimid period, 10th–11th century.
Reproduced by Courtesy of the Trustees of the British Museum

The potting is vigorous but crude, lacking the refinement of the Baghdad ware with its constant references to Chinese models. This may well be in large part due to the coarse and sandy nature of the clay body used. The glazing is haphazard and the tin glaze is also of poor quality, often pitted and a greyish colour. But the decoration is, in comparison with the Abbasid forerunners, quite sophisticated and the range of lustres impressive, extending from pale yellow, khaki and amber through to deep copper reds and browns. In the painting, there is a fresh vigour and diversity stemming from the cultural mix that made up Egyptian civilisation. Whilst some features of the Abbasid designs persist, there is a new-found delight in naturalism (from Greek art) alongside the oriental facility for formal pattern-making; Byzantine and Coptic influences are also visible in the portraits of Christ and the portrayal of birds and fish.

The fact that the forms of the pottery received considerably less attention than the decoration might now point to a division of labour between 'potters', who provide the blanks, and 'painters' who embellish them.[4] This allocation of tasks is traditional throughout the history of decorated tin glaze and is implicitly hierarchical, placing greater importance on the painted decoration than on the form.

There were also some more common, unlustred wares attributed to the Fayyum area near Cairo – painted in a spontaneous fashion with manganese and copper blobs, dots and lines. The Fayyum ware is characterised by its thick, fusible tin glaze, which pools in the middle of bowls, pulling and distorting the painted oxides. Judging from the colour response (copper turquoise and manganese purple) these glazes appear to be alkaline-based. They are also very crazed, probably due both to the high coefficient of expansion of the alkaline glaze and to the sandy, low-expansion body.

Persian lustreware – Rayy and Kashan

These schools represent the last of the line of Middle Eastern tin-glazed ware, at least for several centuries. Both are styles which were closely linked with that of miniature illumination and the illustration of books.

The Seljuk Turks had built up a large empire in the 11th century which included Iran, Iraq and Syria. The prosperity of Seljuk Persia led to a flowering of the arts, and in particular architecture and the applied arts. The Egyptian Fatimid dynasty collapsed in the 12th century and with it the school of lustre painting. The coincidence of a revival of lustred pottery in Persia and Mesopotamia may well be due to the Egyptian craftsmen finding new work under the Seljuk rulers and bringing with them the lustre techniques. The mature quality of the Persian lustres and early stylistic links with Fatimid designs would substantiate this theory. The refined pictorial style which permeated the applied arts indicates a highly sophisticated artistic climate. The subject matter is courtly, poetic and idealised. Caiger-Smith has commented on the mystical and metaphysical overtones of the style.[5] In the depiction of women, there is evidence of a new awareness of femininity. The elegant shapes, of which the ewers, jugs and vases are typical examples, reveal an attention to profile and a fineness of potting not previously seen in Islamic pottery.

Small frit-paste jug, ht 13 cm. Iran (Kashan) late 12th century. Seated figures and foliate motifs. Reddish-brown lustre on tin glaze. Blue glaze inside.
Reproduced by Courtesy of the Trustees of the British Museum

This period saw the combination of lustres on tin glaze with a new kind of body, which had previously been developed by the Seljuk potters. Rayy and Kashan wares were made from a high-silica body known as 'frit-paste', whereby a frit (a type of ground glass composed of alkaline flux and silica) was added to the plastic clay. This process not only made for lower porosity and increased strength, but also created a high-expansion body which cured crazing by putting the glaze under compression. It also produced a whiter, brighter background for the glazes and pigment decoration.

Rayy and Kashan designs are full of rhythm and movement. Typical subjects of decoration are horsemen and moon-faced ladies, with their dotted costumes, surrounded by scrolls, arabesques and swirling foliage. The figures are often enclosed in circles or lined up in frieze formation. The half-moon border, the contour panels and the reserving of figures against a dark background are all devices carried through from the Fatimid and earlier ware, but now underglaze cobalt painting is often combined with the on-glaze lustre work and a blue glaze is also commonly used on the insides of containers.

The sophistication of Rayy ware was taken a stage further in the Kashan potteries[6]: there was meticulous attention to detail and the pot became much more of a vehicle for dense, intricate designs, inspired by textile and book arts. The ever stronger influence of book painting on pottery ornamentation nourished an increasing interest in the decoration of two-dimensional ceramic surfaces. Kashan tile panels, often in star or hexagonal tessellations, were much in demand and were used throughout Persia for the adornment of mosques. In fact, the word 'kashani' became synonymous with tiles and eventually became extended, in the Middle East, to denote any tin-glazed ware, just as Faenza gave its name to faience, Delft to delftware, and Majorca (or Malaga) to maiolica.[7]

Kashan tile with typical 'moon-faced' lady, 13th century. Courtesy of the Board of Trustees of the Victoria and Albert Museum

Minai ware

With Minai ware, also produced by the potters of Rayy and Kashan, we see the first use of enamels on tin glaze.[8] Lustreware has a limited range of colours so it is not surprising that experiments had been underway to find new ways of creating bright colours. Enamels are pigments in the form of low-maturing glazes which are applied to the surface of the fired glaze. They are then hardened on in a third firing to approximately 700–800°C. The low temperature of the enamel firing means that a wide variety of strong colours can be obtained without the volatisation of some oxides which would occur at higher temperatures.

As with the lustre painting of Rayy and Kashan, Minai ware was closely related to the fine miniature painting of illuminated manuscripts. Inspiration also came from contemporary silks. Courtly love and hunting scenes were favourite subjects; other designs were pure

Minai bowl with design of riders, seated figures and sphinxes in a landscape, diam. 20 cm. Kashan, Iran, late 12th century. Enamels on tin glaze.
Reproduced by Courtesy of the Trustees of the British Museum

celebrations of geometric and calligraphic pattern. Painting with enamels was well-suited to the purpose, for it permitted fine detail without fear of distortion or textured fusion with the glaze. It also provided a vastly extended palette of colours which would correspond more closely to the design sources and be more predictable in their outcome. With in-glaze oxide painting, both colours and tonal values change radically from raw to fired state and their intensity is not always easy to gauge. Enamels in their unfired state give a much closer indication of how they will look when fired and there is no interaction between the enamels and the underlying glaze. The whole process therefore is much more controlled (and to many potters also lacking in ceramic excitement). The tin glaze is here not exploited for its inherent qualities but used simply as a white background.

Hispano-Moresque ware

The Arab conquest of Andalucia and other regions of southern Spain was to produce some of the most splendid pots, both lustred and in-glaze painted. The fusion of Eastern and Western cultures brought a new vitality, nobility and flamboyance to the art of vessel-making which was to become a paradigm for decorative earthenware throughout the whole of Europe. The 'Golden Age' of Spanish ceramics began in the mid-13th century with the production at Malaga of tin-glazed, lustred pottery, probably by craftsmen who had come from Egypt, as there were close stylistic links with Fatimid ware. Other important pottery centres were Paterna and Manises (Valencia), Teruel (Aragon), Talavera (Castile) and Catalonia.

The arrival of cobalt ore in Spain round about this time opened up new colour possibilities and in-glaze painting with cobalt was used sometimes on its own, sometimes in combination with lustres. At first the decoration was purely Islamic, but then gradually Christian European imagery crept in. Heraldic shields were juxtaposed with bands of Kufic script, palmettes and other Islamic ornament. Leaf and flower patterns were also popular, often used as 'filler' background to a main motif. This cultural mixture epitomises Hispano-Moresque ware.

Large dish, diam. 44 cm, cobalt blue (painted under the glaze) and gold lustre. Valencia, 1420–1430.
The juxtaposition of Christian and Islamic imagery characteristic of Hispano-Moresque ware is well illustrated here: the Christian coat of arms is that of the royal house of Castile and Leon; the dense surrounding design is composed of purely Islamic elements – the 'tree of life', the 'alafia' script pattern (meaning 'blessing'), spirals, arcs and foliage scrolls.
Reproduced by permission of the Trustees of the Wallace Collection

Some of the Valencian lustred plates and dishes are dazzlingly busy with their dense radiating patterns and it is quite a relief to the eye to move on to the simpler, looser designs which are also characteristic of this period. These sometimes have pride of place on the inside of a bowl (see photograph on p. 20) but are most often to be found on the undersides of the large, densely decorated dishes. The contrast is astonishing. Animal and bird designs, foliage scrolls, scribbles and spirals make maximum use of the available space and are executed in vigorous, calligraphic brushwork.

Other forms of Hispano-Moresque ware reveal a mixed pedigree of Eastern and European influences. Apothecary jars had originated in Mesopotamia, where hospitals and schools of medicine were established. In Europe, these vessels continued to be in demand with an ever-increasing interest in herbal medicine, the publication of pharmacopoeia and the growth of apothecary shops and medical care in general. Containers were required for the storage of

Small bowl, diam. 18 cm. Lustre on tin glaze. Valencia, 15th century.
Bird of prey with stylised acacia foliage and flourishes – a fine example of the vigorous, gestural style of Hispano-Moresque painting. This freer type of painting is often to be found on the undersides of large dishes.
Metropolitan Museum of Art, New York, Rogers Fund, 1913

Albarello, cobalt in-glaze and gold lustre, Valencia 15th century. Reproduced by courtesy of the Trustees of the British Museum

herbs, roots, spices, syrups, ointments. The stability and whiteness of the tin-opacified glaze provided not only a reliable and impervious glaze for these vessels, but also great decorative potential. It was thus that the shapes of the drug jars, and most notably the albarello became closely linked with the tradition of tin-glazed earthenware.

Hispano-Moresque shapes are generous and confident. Apart from the apothecary jars, there were other utilitarian pots – ewers, jugs, basins, buckets and tureens, whose forms related closely to earlier local pottery. There were also wonderful flights of fancy as exemplified in the imposing wing-handled vases and those destined for adornment of special places, for example the Alhambra palace. Most of the flatware shapes derive from beaten metalwork. This can been seen in the angled profiles, domed centres and the common use of relief moulding (later imitated in Italian maiolica, e.g. at Gubbio). These large platters and dishes were probably thrown on to moulds. The embossed centres came to be used as emplacements for jugs.

Another type of Hispano-Moresque ware was developed at Paterna and Teruel. It did not involve the use of lustres. Copper and manganese oxides were used to produce lively designs, most often incorporating human figures, hares, fish, birds and goats. These designs seem to have inherited many features from Fatimid imagery. The brushwork is fluent and the mood, in comparison with the high-status lustreware, is more popular, more European (see also the photograph on p.22).

Quite a different use of tin glaze is manifest in the *cuerda seca* (dry cord) ware, which was developed by Moorish potters in Andalucia. The design was first painted on using oil or fat stained with manganese. The areas in between the lines were then filled in with white and coloured tin glazes. The fat burned out in the firing leaving a dark, dry line of separation between the different colours. The technique at first lent itself to mosaic-like patterns in white, green and brown on tiles, and later to stronger designs with larger glazed areas of white, blue, black and amber on wide shallow bowls (see photograph on p.23). Unfortunately the separation idea was not always that effective, particularly as the large dishes were fired on their sides, thereby encouraging the flow of colour from one compartment to the next. There was another technique for separating areas of coloured glazes, known as *cuenca*, which involved the use of *cloisonné*-type clay walls. This was commonly used in tile production.

Hispano-Moresque ware was much in demand in 15th-century Europe and it was

Winged vase, ht 52 cm, cobalt blue in-glaze and gold lustre. Valencia, 15th century.
Design of vine, bryony and acacia leaves.
Courtesy of the Board of Trustees of the Victoria and Albert Museum

Dish, manganese brown and copper green painting. Paterna 13th–14th century.
The design derives from the Egyptian repertoire.
Museo de Ceramica, Barcelona

widely exported. Large numbers of pots have been excavated in London, Bristol and the Low Countries.[10] But it was the Italian nobility which especially aspired to possession of these highly-valued wares. Commemorative and armorial pieces were specially commissioned. Some of the jugs were copies of Tuscan shapes and bore Italian family insignia, but were otherwise decorated with pure Hispano-Moresque ornament. However, gradually, the Italians turned their patronage to their own potters who were beginning to produce pots which were highly decorative, less expensive and more in keeping with the classical, humanist ideals of the time. The Spanish ware was now too Islamic in feel for the tastes of Renaissance Italy. In Spain, production of lustreware began to decline. The next creative impetus for tin glaze in Spain was to come on the rebound from Italy, but this did not occur until the 16th century (see p. 60).

Notes

1 Allan, J.W., *Islamic Ceramics*, Oxford (Ashmolean Museum, 1991)
2 Cobalt was referred to by the Chinese as 'Mohammedan blue'
3 Caiger-Smith, A., *Tin-glaze Pottery in Europe and the Islamic World*, London (Faber and Faber, 1973)
4 ibid.
5 Caiger-Smith, A., *Lustre Pottery*, London (Faber and Faber, 1985); now also in paperback (Herbert Press)
6 Dr James Allan informs me that latest opinion now considers Rayy lustre to be the early version of Kashan, i.e. it was made in Kashan too.
7 as 3
8 Minai ware so called after the Arabic word *mina* = glaze, J.Allan, op. cit.
9 Illustrated in his book, *The Potter's Challenge*, London (Souvenir Press, 1976)
10 Wilson, T., *Ceramic Art of the Italian Renaissance*, London (British Museum, 1987)

Large 'cuerda seca' dish, Seville, first half of the 16th century.
Courtesy of the Board of Trustees of the Victoria and Albert Museum

Plate, diam approx 25 cm. manganese brown and copper green painting. Teruel, 15th–16th century.
The glaze has been thickly applied causing pronounced texturing of the manganese pigment. The hare was a popular motif in Islamic pottery. This particular design was much admired by Bernard Leach who imitated it in his early career.[9]
Courtesy of the Board of Trustees of the Victoria and Albert Museum

Italian Maiolica

The imported Spanish lustreware became known in Italy as 'maiolica', probably a corruption of 'Majorca', an important port for trade between Spain and Italy at that time, although it could also derive from the Spanish *obra de malaga* (Malaga work, i.e. lustreware).[1] The term maiolica at first referred only to lustreware, Spanish and Italian; it later came to be used as a generic term for tin-glazed earthenware. Italy was the pivotal point from which maiolica with its new-found status in the decorative arts, was to spread throughout Europe and even further afield.

Tin-glazed earthenware as developed by the Italians is extraordinary in the history of ceramics for its elevation almost to the ranks of the fine arts. The tremendous potential for colour on tin-glaze ware was no doubt partly responsible for its new status. The decorators of the pots were also quick to pick up on both subject matter and style of Renaissance painting, the smooth white surface of the glaze inviting refinements of tone and line; in later maiolica, and particularly in the *istoriato*, or narrative, pieces, we see the phenomenon of pottery being treated as a form of pure painting.

Archaic maiolica

To me it is the early expressions of maiolica, when pots were made primarily to be used, which communicate the most strength of feeling in their simplicity of concept. Alas, and because of their domestic function, fewer examples of these have survived intact than the later ornamental ware. What is now known as 'archaic maiolica' was already being produced in Italy as early as the 11th and 12th centuries. The very earliest examples have been excavated at sites which were once Crusader strongholds in Southern Italy and Sicily.

The production of tin-glazed ware was quite established by the middle of the 13th century, particularly in Tuscany and Umbria. The tin-glazed pottery was more costly than the ubiquitous lead-glazed slipware but it was still affordable for the middle classes, the hostelries and the monasteries. Tin oxide was, even in those days, an expensive commodity, and much of it was imported from Devon and Cornwall. Many of the pots were glazed with the tin glaze only on the visible surfaces, the underneaths and insides being covered with a clear lead glaze. Large quantities of this archaic maiolica ware were dug up in Orvieto before the First World War and were promptly pillaged by museums and collectors. This early ware is often also referred to as 'Orvieto ware'.

Some of the shapes referred back directly to the Islamic tradition, notably the albarello and other drug-jar shapes, but now distinctive Italian forms were beginning to emerge. These are most evident in the jugs: typical examples are the pear-shaped pedestal jug, the *panata* with a thrown and applied lip (see photographs on p. 25) and the loosely-shaped trilobate jugs. The characteristic wide, flat, strap-like handle with a sharp change of angle in the profile also began to appear. Dishes and flatware shapes were still based on metalwork prototypes. Decoration was strikingly sparse, dictated by the shape, and it often gave the impression of playing with lines. Many of the designs derived from Islamic metalwork;[2] others depicted plant forms, animals and coats of arms. Cross-hatched lines are frequently used as

Panata (jug with applied spout), ht 14.8 cm, Umbria 14th century.
Painted in manganese and copper. Lower part and interior are lead-glazed. A simple, whimsical gesture is the only decoration on this piece.
Museo del Vino, Torgiano, Lungarotti Foundation

Pedestal jug, painted in manganese and copper, Orvieto district, 14th century.
Reproduced by Courtesy of the Trustees of the British Museum

groundwork to give prominence to the main design feature. The painting, as with all subsequent Italian maiolica, was pictorial and line-based. The brush was used as tool for description, rather than exploited for its innate qualities of stroke. As to composition – even in the non-representational, geometric designs, the frame of visual reference was that of a picture plane. The palette was restricted to manganese brown and copper green and may well have been influenced by the colours of the locally produced lead-glazed slipware. There are also obvious parallels with the browns and greens of the contemporary Spanish Paterna ware.

New developments in Tuscany

The first signs of any significant developments appeared soon after 1400 in Tuscany, when some large, deep dishes began to be made in Florence. They still employed the archaic Umbrian palette of brown and green, but now were distinctly Gothic in feel and quite sophisticated in comparison with what had gone before. The label 'severe' sometimes used to describe the various Tuscan styles of this period is somewhat of a misnomer; it would appear to refer to the simplicity of shape and decoration and the use of a limited range of colours. However, in comparison with the archaic period, these wares were considerably more mature in design and richer of palette, as they now included yellow and blue.

It is in this first group of work – *la famiglia verde* – that the first attempts were made to imitate contemporary painting. The portrait on the dish on p.26 closely resembles the style of portraits painted by, for example, Piero della Francesca, Botticelli and Antonio Pollaiolo. The hare portrayed on another dish could be an enlarged detail from the background of any of the early Renaissance paintings. Florence was the hub of artistic activity at this time, so it is not surprising that this is where the impact of painting first became apparent in pottery. Influenced by painting, ceramic decoration began to incorporate graded tones of colour to suggest depth and form. Yet the influence was not so powerful as to dominate, and articulation of three-dimensional form still played an important part in the overall concept.

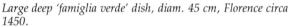

Large deep 'famiglia verde' dish, diam. 45 cm, Florence circa 1450.
Painted in manganese, copper and antimony yellow, with faint touches of blue. The shape and the flower and foliage patterning may relate closely to Hispano-Moresque ware but the influence of early Renaissance portraiture is undeniable and there is a new-found finesse in the painting. Note the continued convention of the Islamic contour panel.
Courtesy of the Board of Trustees of the Victoria and Albert Museum

'Oak-leaf' drug jar, Florence 15th century.
Blue pigment (possibly blue glaze) with manganese outlines on tin glaze. Many of the motifs from the archaic period continue to appear on this type of ware.
Fitzwilliam Museum, Cambridge

Another quite distinctive type of ware was also produced in Florence at that time – the relief-blue, 'oak-leaf' drug jars and jugs. Many of the jars were barrel-shaped, with short necks and two strap handles. The main subject of decoration – for example, human figure, bird, heraldic lion or coat of arms, was set against a background of indented leaves (resembling oak leaves) and stalks. The strong influence of Valencian decoration, both in colour scheme and leaf-patterned ground is obvious, although many of the motifs – birds, lions, fish – bear a strong relation to contemporary textile designs.[3] The outlines were drawn in manganese-purple and filled in with a rich dark blue pigment. This stood out in relief from the white ground and had the appearance of a glaze. It was most probably cobalt, then a very impure oxide and therefore quite refractory, mixed with a flux such as raw lead (e.g. litharge) or even the tin base-glaze. Most of these wares were made for hospitals and pharmacies and the scale of production

was impressive. A contract made in 1430 records an order for 1,000 jars of various shapes and sizes placed by the Florence hospital of Santa Maria Nuova with the workshop of a Florentine potter, Giunta di Tugio.[4]

Faenza and the 'Italo-Moresque' style

The last half of the 15th century saw the ascendancy of Faenza and several other maiolica workshops in Northern and Central Italy and exciting new developments in the way of colour and decoration. These distinctive new designs set the mood for the subsequent development of Italian maiolica and their influence can be seen right through to Flemish and English tin-glaze ware. The ornament was characterised by its vigour and vibrant colours. Much of the decorative vocabulary derived from Valencian Hispano-Moresque ware – the leaf and flower patterns, the Persian palmette, the pine cone, arabesques and scrolls; the convention of the contour panel was also adopted and adapted to new shapes and imagery. But new elements were also appearing – characteristic of Faenza designs were the broad scrolled 'split' leaves, divided into two areas of colour, the peacock eye, which lent itself so well to repeat patterning, the wavy rays (in homage to St Bernardino of Siena) and classical features from architecture and sculpture. This fully mature Faenza style is often referred to as 'Gothic-Floral' although, again, this seems an inadequate appellation and does not convey the boldness and visual impact of the designs.

The main output continued to be drug jars in their various forms but there was also great demand for commemorative wares, marking betrothals, marriages, births. These commonly portray people and incorporate appropriate sayings or proverbs, exemplifying an ever increasing adoption of Humanist ideas in emulation of the major arts.

Form and decoration were well-balanced.

Plate, Faenza 1470–80.
Painted in blue, green, yellow, orange and manganese purple. The inscription reads 'My heart is wounded for you'. The peacock-eye, floral scrolls and dots are typica! of this period of fusion of Hispano-Moresque and Renaissance ornament.
Courtesy of the Board of Trustees of the Victoria and Albert Museum

Albarellos, ht. 13.4 and 13.6 cm, probably Siena circa 1500–1510.
An elegant combination of patterns and colours.
Ashmolean Museum, Oxford

Two-handled albarello, ht 21.8 cm, Tuscany, possibly Florence third quarter of the 15th century.
Painted in cobalt blue, antimony yellow, manganese purple and copper green. The coat of arms, framed with characteristic broad scrolled 'split' leaves, is probably that of the Florentine Gianfigliazzi family. The neck is decorated with the wavy rays of 'San Bernardino'. The handles are a curious reiteration of those on Hispano-Moresque vases (see illus. page 21), but here they are painted in manganese and the fine white line is sgraffitoed through the pigment to the underlying glaze.
Reproduced by permission of the Trustees of the Wallace Collection

Areas to be decorated were usually organised to give a structure to the design; cylindrical albarellos, for example, were often divided into panels or bands, the necks and feet treated with a variety of geometric borders or simple banding. Fat-bellied jugs and jars usually bore the main decorative element at the centre front and this was framed with a contour panel of, for example, bands or garlands, which harmonised with the shape of the pot and separated it from a more loosely decorated background area.

The numerous new religious and secular buildings being built also gave fresh impetus to the potters, who were now working closely with the designers to provide architectural ceramics such as wall roundels, tile panels and pavements to enhance both interiors and exteriors. There is a tiled pavement, made at Faenza in 1487 for the church of San Petronio, Bologna, which in itself constitutes a wonderful source of reference for contemporary decorative vocabulary.

Great technical progress was also made at Faenza. The glaze had an opacity and sheen previously unknown. The palette of colours was brilliantly extended to a powerful and complimentary grouping. Predominant was a dark rich blue (for lines, outlines, backgrounds) offset by a soft turquoise copper green, a rich manganese purple, an egg yellow (lead antimonate) and a rusty orange (lead antimonate and iron oxide). In addition, cobalt was used in very diluted form as a shaded wash, often as a base for finer, darker, scribbly lines. These pigments formed the basic colour grouping that is so characteristic of Italian and Italianate maiolica.

Quite a separate ceramic phenomenon was meanwhile developing in the Florentine workshop of Luca della Robbia (1400–1482); the glazed terracotta reliefs of the della Robbia family – lunettes, roundels, armorial medallions – are directly descended from the *bas-relief* sculptural traditions of Ghiberti and Donatello and were quite separate from the activities of the maiolica potters. Nevertheless, their influence

Jug, Faenza, late 15th or early 16th century.
The framed bust of a woman in Renaissance costume was a popular form of ornament.
Museo Internazionale delle Ceramiche, Faenza

was felt in the pottery workshops, which were beginning not only to embellish their pots with modelled details but also to make more individual pieces that did not necessarily have a utilitarian function – plaques, free-standing figures, busts etc. Bowls of imitation fruit were a Faenza speciality in the 16th century. Luca della Robbia himself started out as a highly successful sculptor in stone, marble and bronze, one of his earliest achievements being the Cantoria in the Duomo, Florence with its panels of expressive musicians. The first appearance of ceramics in his work is on the Peretola Tabernacle (1441) in the form of polychrome-glazed garlands of fruit and flowers, white-glazed cherub heads and blue-glazed background. All of these features were to become hallmarks of the della Robbia workshop. From then on, he worked almost exclusively in glazed terracotta. Possible reasons for the change of medium include economy, speed of execution and durability of colours. It has also been suggested[5] that Brunelleschi, architect of many buildings in Florence where Luca was also concerned with decoration, promoted the use of glazed terracotta as a means of extra enrichment of his designs. Luca's nephew, Andrea, and Andrea's son Giovanni continued the tradition and maintained a prolific output well into the 16th century, although much of the freshness and simplicity of Luca's creations was lost in a more conventionalised approach.

The della Robbias' use of tin glaze was only occasionally as a base for oxide painting (as, for example, in their infrequent production of tiles). The tin glaze was most often used on its own to cover whole figures, which stood out against a sky-blue background. This background was itself the same tin glaze coloured with cobalt. Other coloured glazes used were green, brown and yellow, which were typically applied to the garlanded borders.

Dragon-spouted drug jar, ht 27.5 cm, Faenza 1515.
Inscribed *syo de abscitio* (syrup of absinth), painted in blue, yellow, orange-rust and green. The central subject, a partly-draped man reclining between two naked, crowned women, is flanked by green leaves on a blue ground. The blue scrolls and zig-zags at the back have been painted in very casual manner.
Courtesy of the Board of Trustees of the Victoria and Albert Museum

Vase of fruit, flowers and vegetables, ht 34.5 cm. Della Robbia workshop, Florence, c. 1490–1520.
The vase (whose handles are now missing) is glazed in blue tin glaze with traces of gilding; the top is painted with yellow, green, purple and blue.
Reproduced by courtesy of the Trustees of the British Museum

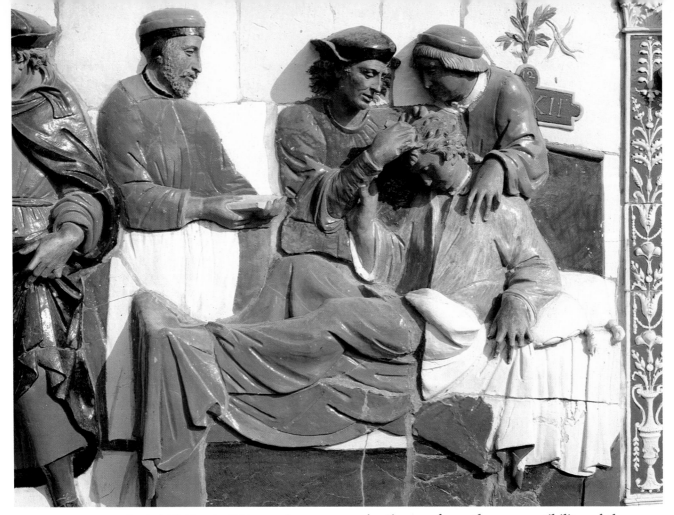

Giovanni della Robbia, detail of 'Visiting the Sick', part of a frieze illustrating the Seven Works of Mercy, 1526–28, Ospedale del Ceppo, Pistoia.
White and coloured tin glazes on terracotta. Set between the pillars of the arcades, this frieze occupied the last years of Giovanni's life. It is more personal and expressive than the main body of often quite conventionalised work produced by this later della Robbia workshop.
Photograph by Aurelio Amendola

Istoriato maiolica

With the flowering of the Renaissance in the early 16th century, the status of the fine-artist painter was supreme. Any process involving manual or mechanical work was considered fairly contemptible. Pottery too was susceptible to the prevailing climate and the ceramic painters were keen to shake themselves free of being perceived as mere craftsmen. Pictorial considerations began to take precedence over those of function and form, giving rise to the emergence of showpieces – elaborately decorated individual pieces, now often signed and dated by the artist. It was no longer sufficient for the ceramic painter to paint from his own im-

agination or from the suggestibility of the contours of the pot. Imagery was now only valued if it were borrowed from a respected source, be it the Bible, Classical mythology or legend, or copied from prints by or after such artists as Raphael, Dürer or Mantegna. These narrative pieces, prototypes of which were perhaps first developed in Faenza in the late 15th century or early 1500s, are referred to as *istoriato* maiolica. Urbino and Castel Durante subsequently became the most important producers of the genre, known for their skilled painters such as Nicola da Urbino and Francesco Xanto Avelli. As pots increasingly became mere vehicles for decoration, so the traditional variety of pottery forms was pared down to those that most resembled canvasses. Most of the *istoriato* dishes and plates were decorated across the whole surface despite the persistence of rims which must have hindered the painter. The art of the ceramic painter was directed at astounding the viewer with his virtuosity. The more intricate the content the more impressive it was. The painter was considered of higher status than the pot maker, and *istoriato* wares are identified in terms of who painted them rather than who made them.

Istoriato ware represented only a small proportion of the ceramic output but because of its non-utilitarian nature, relatively large numbers have survived in good condition.

Large istoriato dish, diam. 54 cm, portraying the conversion of Saul. Probably Urbino, circa 1545.
Painted in blue, yellow, green, orange, brown, purple, grey, black, white. An ambitious composition of full-blown Mannerist persuasion, inspired by Michelangelo's painting of the same subject in the Capella Paolina in the Vatican. The dense, complex composition and dramatic 'story' are characteristic of High Renaissance *istoriato*.
Reproduced by courtesy of the Trustees of the British Museum

It is easy today to be critical of this pictorial, derivative approach to decoration, which tended to work against the plastic qualities of the support. Through Modernist eyes, it can be seen as an alienation from the true business of ceramic design – the decoration an irrelevant imposition, not an articulation of form. Philip Rawson[6] comments on the visual contradictions created by *istoriato*-type perspective imagery on pots, which

> . . . demand(s) that we read into the pot some kind of space which is not limited to its own surface . . . Using emphatic and relatively intractable ceramic glaze substances in strongly conventional colours, (the maiolica pictures) set out to imitate typical three-dimensional

techniques of Renaissance relief-sculpture and painting which were based upon that monocular peephole-perspective which subordinates figures to a horizon line and a unified vanishing point. This creates the visual illusion of a continuous 'space-box' which . . . begins at the foreground and ends at a deep horizon. . . . This drastic conflict between conceptual space and emphatic glaze surfaces with their constant colour system can produce a most extraordinary and disturbing effect. . . . converting the surfaces of pottery into analogues of conventional painting supports which were supposed virtually to abolish themselves in favour of the depth-boxes painted onto them.

However, it should be remembered that at the height of the *istoriato* period of maiolica from the 1520s onwards, the shift of taste brought about by Mannerist painting had affected basic attitudes throughout the decorative arts. John Shearman in his illuminating book *Mannerism*[7] describes some of the qualities valued during that period, many of which are applicable to the appreciation of *istoriato* maiolica in its context:

> virtuosity, facility, refinement, stylisation, complexity, obscurity, variety, abundance, density, capricious use of compositional devices – e.g. legitimate artistic adaptation of proportion and perspective, the absolute work of art.

Other types of High Renaissance ornament

There was also in use a whole category of fantasy decoration based on motifs derived from ancient Rome. Roman grotto paintings had been popularised by Raphael's decoration of the Vatican Loggias, and gave rise to a wave of 'grotesque' decoration featuring bizarre winged creatures, swans, satyrs, bearded heads, garlands, skulls, vases, draperies and such like. Other classical motifs included trophies of arms, books, musical instruments, cupids, dolphins and rabbits. This type of decoration was often used on the wide flat rims of *tondini* to enclose a central pictorial medallion (see photograph below). The background was sometimes white, but coloured grounds were also popular. Faenza in particular developed the use of coloured tin glazes – ranging from a rich dark blue to the off-white of *bianco sopra bianco* and the lavender blue of the *berretino*. These coloured grounds were decorated with opaque white and pastel tin-based pigments.

Lustreware was developed at two main centres – Deruta and Gubbio – from about 1500 onwards. Deruta, still an important pottery centre today, was probably the first in Italy to master the technique of lustre painting, and is known for its distinctive silvery-yellow lustre, often used with in-glaze cobalt painting. Characteristic of Deruta are the large plates with patterned borders incorporating the fish-scale motif. The use of the lustre as a filler, gives a flatter, more graphically simplistic quality to the designs. Huntsmen and portraits of women were among the most usual designs and there was considerable stylistic influence from local Umbrian painters such as Pintoricchio and Perugino. The proximity of Assisi, with its cult of St Francis, also meant that religious subjects were popular.[2]

Tondino, diam. 23.8 cm, Castel Durante (attributed to the workshop of Giovanni Maria), circa 1515.
The wide rim is painted, in tan, yellow and green, with trophies of arms and books, cornucopias, musical instruments, dolphins, rabbits and scrolls on a midnight blue ground. The reverse of the piece is, typically, decorated with groups of concentric blue circles.
Reproduced by permission of the Trustees of the Wallace Collection

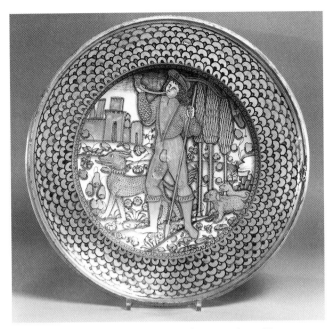

Dish, a huntsman blowing his horn, diam. 42.4 cm, Deruta, circa 1500–1530.
Blue in-glaze painting and gold lustre. The naive perspective, flat colours and dominant use of pattern contribute to the attractive simplicity of Deruta wares.
Ashmolean Museum, Oxford

Gubbio also became famous for its production of lustred tin-glaze ware, which was developed by Maestro Georgio Andreoli. The embossed and gadrooned forms of Gubbio ware echo their Hispano-Moresque ancestors, and the lustre palette is dominated by a rich ruby red.

Venice has always had quite a separate development in the fine arts and architecture. Venetian maiolica was refreshingly different from the mainstream Tuscan/Umbrian ware, chiefly due to its being more accessible, as an important trading port, to influences from the Middle and Far East. The Isnik style inspired many of its flower designs and there were some wonderful large rounded jars decorated with luscious fruit and foliage (see photograph on p.35). Their delicate *alla porcellana* designs reflected those on oriental porcelain, and were painted in white on a blue-tinted base glaze. The Venetian technique of glazing was also different. Whereas the mainstream High Renaissance maiolica (as described by Piccolpasso) employed a matt white base (*bianco*) for painting and covered it with a transparent overglaze (*coperta*), Venetian potteries painted directly on to a single fusible tin glaze.

The latter half of the 16th century saw the inevitable decline of *istoriato* and other High Renaissance conventions which could no longer compete with the stylistic extremes of Mannerism. Designs had become mass-produced and conventionalised. Tin-glazed earthenware began to find other means of expression. The *bianchi* (whitewares) of Faenza, with their relief moulding, piercing and minimal painted decoration were a welcome relief from the busyness of *istoriato*. In other painted wares a new more spontaneous sketchy (*compendario*) style emerged, as exemplified in the lively Montelupo designs of women, soldiers and bandits. Montelupo is also known for its vigorous geometric designs (see photographs on pp. 34, 36 and 61).

Albarello with relief moulding, ht 23.5 cm, Gubbio, circa 1510.
Painted in-glaze with copper and cobalt. The gadroons, indentations and the grooves on the handles are picked out in ruby lustre.
Courtesy of the Board of Trustees of the Victoria and Albert Museum

There is no shortage of technical information about ceramic production in 16th century Italy, thanks to Cipriano Piccolpasso, an observer of pottery-making (and possibly amateur potter himself?) who lived in Urbino. In his treatise, *The Three Books of the Potter's Art* written circa 1558, he documents all aspects of pottery production

*Dish, diam. 33.6 cm, probably Montelupo, 1500–1530. Painted
in blue, green, red, yellow.*
Reproduced by courtesy of the Trustees of the British Museum

*Large jar, ht approx. 30 cm. Most probably Venice early 16th
century.*
Courtauld Institute Galleries

that were known to him – making methods, glaze and pigment recipes, kiln designs and firing techniques, as well as giving clear illustrations of all the popular design patterns of the time. The basic materials and techniques of Italian maiolica as described by Piccolpasso are discussed in Section II.

From Italy, the fashion for decorated tin glaze spread throughout Europe. In the early 1500s, Italian potters, with an eye to new and developing markets and fresh stimulus, started to emigrate and set up workshops, initially in Spain, France, Antwerp and later in Switzerland. From Antwerp, the technique travelled to Holland, to Germany (via Holland) and England. From Switzerland, it was to move eastwards to Austria, Bohemia, Moravia, Slovakia and Hungary. In each of these countries, the style of work was at the outset predominantly Italian, but gradually regional characteristics began to creep in and new, distinct styles emerged.

Notes

1 This is an endless debate. According to Wilson, most of the early Italian documents include the 'o' indicating that the island of Majorca was being referred to rather than Malaga.
2 Miss Julia Poole of Fitzwilliam Museum, verbal communication
3 Ibid.
4 Wilson, Timothy, *Ceramic Art of the Italian Renaissance*, London (British Museum, 1987)
5 Pope-Hennessy, Sir John, *Luca Della Robbia*, London (Phaidon, 1980)
6 Rawson, Philip, *Ceramics*, London (Oxford University Press, 1971)
7 Shearman, John, *Mannerism*, London (Pelican, 1967). Now available as a Penguin paperback.

Portrait dish on a low foot, diam. 26.7 cm, Castel Durante 1525–1550.
Painted in blue, yellow, orange, green, grey and opaque white on a brilliant blue ground. The clarity of the lines and high shine of the glaze may well indicate use of the transparent overglaze or *coperta*. These dishes with portraits of beautiful young women were very popular and are generally thought to have been gifts of love (*coppe amatorie*) from men to their beloveds, although it is also possible the more classical names refer to literary ladies rather than real-life ones (*cf.* T. Wilson, 1987).
Reproduced by permission of the Trustees of the Wallace Collection

Spouted jar, ht. 38 cm, Asciano, 1600.
The handle and details are painted in blue, yellow, green, rust-brown and purple. The arms are those of Palmieri of Siena. Whitewares (*bianchi*) began to be made in Faenza about 1540 and became immensely popular not only in Italy but all over Europe; they marked the beginning of the fashion for tin-glazed tableware. The dimpled wall is a feature which was readily adopted in other European whitewares, e.g. Lambeth.
Reproduced by courtesy of the Trustees of the British Museum

French Faience

Most of the tin-glazed ware made in France in the 16th century closely resembled the Italian models – not surprising, as it was initially made by Italian potters, and later by Frenchmen schooled by the Italians. Italian potters were already working in France in the 1520s and in 1525 some of them were employed, under the orders of Marguerite of Flanders, in the making of a tiled pavement in the Cathedral of Brou. A Frenchman called Masseot Abaquesne was probably working with the Italians on the project, having previously worked with Girolamo della Robbia (of the Florentine family) on architectural ceramics for the Château de Madrid in Paris. After Brou, Abaquesne went on to found his own pottery at Rouen, where he continued his architectural work alongside production of drug jars in the Italianate style (see photograph on p.38). Other potteries were set up in Lyons and Nîmes and produced pots in *istoriato* and High Renaissance styles. Italians also settled in Nevers, which became the first city to transmute the Italian maiolica painting tradition into something entirely French in character, although this did not really occur until well into the 17th century. This new, very French style – a product of the joint influences of Baroque art and Chinese porcelain – which evolved at Nevers was to permeate other faience centres, such as Rouen, Moustiers and Marseilles, until virtually the beginning of the 18th century.

The term 'faience' came to be used in France to denote tin-glazed earthenware in the late 16th century. It derived from *bianchi di Faenza* – the whitewares which began to be produced in Faenza about 1550 in direct reaction to the glut of densely-decorated *istoriato* pots. The fashion spread to France (as well as Flanders and Central Europe); these plain or very simply decorated pots for mass consumption and everyday use were cheap to market, became very popular and also allowed the factories the luxury of producing highly decorated ware for more sophisticated customers. This dual tradition continued on throughout the history of French faience, the simpler *faience populaire* being made by country potteries well into the 19th century.

The Nevers faience industry was started in the late 16th century by the Conrade brothers from Albisola in Italy. They had been brought to Nevers by Luigi dei Gonzaga, who had become Duke of Nivernais through his marriage to Henrietta of Cleves in 1565. A royal privilege was granted to the Conrades by Henri IV, giving them exclusive rights of faience production for 30 years. Not only did they make the usual forms and designs of drug jars, decorative plates etc. in Italianate style, but also produced glazed sculptural pieces in the Della Robbia tradition.

By 1630, other factories were beginning to set up in the area. The Italian style persisted until the end of the century but French overtones began to creep in. The early Louis XIV Baroque taste for the rotund and the grandiose is evident in both the architecture and the painting of the time, and in turn filters through to the faience and other applied arts. In painting, a national style was already emerging in the works of Poussin, Le Brun and Simon Vouet. They had all made 'pilgrimages' to Rome and were steeped in the Classical spirit although they tempered the excesses of Italian Baroque and their compositions were simpler. The faience decorators turned their attention to the engravings of Poussin, Van Dyck, Vouet and other contemporary artists published by Michel Dorigny in the 1640s. The curvacious forms of the ware derive

Two views of a spouted jar (chevrette), ht 21 cm.,
by Masseot Abaquesne, Rouen, 1545
Although the design of a profile bust surrounded by a
wreath and foliage scrolls is essentially Faentine, the
painting is looser and more naturalistic.
Musée Nationale de la Céramique, Sèvres, photograph © RMN
1993

chiefly from Baroque silver of the time. Arthur
Lane[1] describes the Nevers faience of the time
as characterised by a 'cheerful blowsiness'.
Although the influence of the fine arts was still
supreme, there was now evidence of a little
more concern for the three-dimensional qualities
of the pots. The 'picture' no longer covered the
whole surface of a dish, regardless of its contours, but was confined within emblematic borders which followed the shape. Areas of pots
were divided up in architectural fashion, providing a framework for sequences of designs. The
drawing, compared with say Italian High
Renaissance maiolica, was unsophisticated. In
contrast to the earlier Italianate ware, the colours
and lines had an attractive softness deriving
partly from the thickness of the glaze application
and a relatively high firing. The glossy milkiness
of the glaze and the marked breaking up of the
pigment is attributed by Caiger-Smith[2] to a high
lime content in the glaze composition.

Another important stylistic influence now also
came via Holland from the East. Chinese Ming
porcelain began to be exported to Europe via the
Dutch East India Company in the 17th century
and its impact spread like wildfire to every area
of the decorative arts. In ceramics, and at Nevers
in particular, we can now see an extraordinary
juxtaposition of Baroque and Chinese styles.
Baroque pastoral scenes were imposed on pure
Ming shape vases; Chinese 'blue and white'
designs adorned ceramic forms based on contemporary French metalwork. Any borrowing
was permissible. At its best, Nevers 'Chinese'
ware has a clumsy charm. There is a particularly
attractive shape of double-bulged or onion vase
which was often used for Ming-type scenes of
figures in a landscape. The glaze was thickly
applied and tinted a milky pale blue. The decoration was executed in shades of cobalt blue and
outlined in manganese purple.

Peculiar to Nevers, and later much imitated
elsewhere, were the *bleu de Nevers* (sometimes
mistakenly referred to as *bleu persan*) designs,
predominantly oriental in mood with flowers,
leaves and birds delicately painted in opaque
white and yellow pigments on a dark blue glaze
(tin glaze stained with cobalt). This technique
may well have come from the blue grounds of
Castelli, Faenza and Venice. In comparison, the
Nevers version seems rather lifeless, lacking in
both surface quality and visual dynamics.

By the 18th century, the creativity of the
Nevers *faienceries* was already in decline and
threatened by the innovative designs of Rouen
and Moustiers. From then on the Nevers potters
concentrated on producing simple, *faience
blanche* wares for everyday use, and they became
particularly known for their *faiences parlantes* –

plates and other wares bearing inscriptions of a moral, satirical, humorous or political nature.

Up until the 18th century, faience had been destined for pharmacies, architectural ornament or ceremonial wares. *Faience blanche* was used as tableware, but only by the bourgeoisie; the nobility were still eating off gold or silver. Two important events towards the end of the 17th century changed the whole course of French faience. One was the construction in 1670 of the Trianon de Porcelaine, commissioned by Louis XIV for his mistress Madame de Montespan. It was in fact a *trianon de faience*, the reference to porcelain being in homage to the Chinese export ware which was held in such great esteem at the time. The roof, outer walls and floors were entirely covered with tiles from Delft, Rouen and Nevers; the colour scheme was, naturally enough, blue and white. Although it did not withstand the ravages of time and the weather, it brought faience to the attention of a much wider public.

The other and more decisive catalyst for the growth of faience as a highly fashionable commodity came at the turn of the century. After the prolonged wars waged by Louis XIV, the Treasury was seriously depleted. In a series of edicts, issued between 1689 and 1709, all gold and silver belonging to the nobility was ordered to be melted down to boost the coffers. Suddenly faience was gracing all the best banqueting tables. According to Saint-Simon in his *Mémoires* of 1709, 'every man of any status or consequence turned within a week to faience'. French faience was to remain at the peak of fashionability and dominant in Europe throughout the greater part of the 18th century.

The precipitate adoption of faience as smart tableware produced a lightning expansion of the industry. Demand was enormous, and it was met by new factories and increasingly streamlined processes. Many shapes were now pressmoulded for ease of repetition, reducing the need for skilled throwers and modellers. The extent and range of the wares increased considerably. Designs, often to commission, were created for mass production which could be carried out by trained but essentially non-creative decorators. Glaze quality improved to new hygienic standards. The importance of the artist in creating designs was already diminishing in deference to technical skill and sheer dexterity.

Lidded jar, ht 32 cm, Nevers circa 1630–70.
Painted in blue, green, yellow, orange, grey, purple, black. Mythical marine scenarios (here Europa and the Bull) on a background of blue waves derived from prints by Michel Dorigny and Pierre Brébiette were a popular form of ornament on Nevers pieces. The baluster shape hints at Chinese origins.
Reproduced by courtesy of the Trustees of the British Museum

In keeping with French cultural tradition, and in contrast to Italian Renaissance maiolica, faience was first and foremost designed to be functional, albeit highly decorative, tableware which would complement and enhance the serious business of eating and drinking. This is readily ascertained by a glance at the tremendous range of items made by the faienceries: ice pails, sugar casters, sauceboats, teapots, mustard pots and wine ewers. There were soup tureens to hold the place of honour in the centre of the table, which were often themselves placed on raised *surtouts de table*; Rouen made some huge and impressive table trays (quite a technical achievement) and the largest of their dishes could hold 'twelve to fifteen chickens' or 'eighteen to twenty partridges'! Faience was also increasingly used for architectural accessories such as wall brackets, and for home furnishings such as clocks, water cisterns and globes.

Ewer, ht 28 cm, Rouen 1725.
Blue and white. The shape is from the silver tableware that faience was so rapidly supplanting. Restrained, orderly classicism of form and decoration is typical of 18th century Rouen.
Musée Nationale de la Céramique, Sèvres © *RMN 1993*

The cooler, more academic designs of Rouen faience came into being as part of a generalised reaction to the extravagant dynamics of the Baroque movement and reflect very much the elegant, classicising style of late 17th-century France. The 1668 enlargement of Versailles led the way in its concern with lightness, precision and symmetry. The faience of Rouen was distinctive in its ability to embody in ceramics this new aesthetic climate. Architectural themes were echoed in its straight lines and repetitive ornament; the *style rayonnant*, with intricate, often radiating designs incorporating Baroque motifs and *lambrequins*, derived from Renaissance ornament and could also be seen in contemporary wrought ironwork, fabrics and other applied arts. The small scale of the design units also meant that they could easily be adapted to fit the tremendous variety of shapes.[3]

At first, the Rouen palette was predominantly blue and white, in accordance with the Delft-Chinese mode. Edmé Poterat's factory was established in 1647, almost 80 years after the closure of Abaquesne's workshop. It supplied blue and white tiles and vases for the Trianon de Porcelaine. This colour scheme was also preferred by the nobility for their armorial dinner services. From about 1715, subtle touches of yellow (antimony), green (copper or copper and antimony) and an attractive iron red, similar in colour to the Armenian 'bole' red used on Isnik ware, began to be added to offset the strong blues. This brick red was made from red ochre which contained haematite, the purest form of ferric oxide (Fe_2O_3). The clay content of the ochre would account for the slight roughness of the pigment after firing. It is very difficult to achieve this type of high-firing red today as the commercially available red ochres obviously do not have the same composition and tend to produce dull browns. It might be worth experimenting with naturally occurring ochres (e.g. from the Lubéron in Provence).

Lane[4] speaks of the 'thick, heavy and clumsy' potting of Rouen ware but it seems to me that this, very relative, crudeness is honest and straightforward and very much part of their appeal.

The 18th century saw the flourishing of four main schools – Rouen, Moustiers, Marseilles and Strasbourg, and a vast number of smaller potteries throughout France emulating their

Jug, ht 21 cm. Olerys and Laugier factory, Moustiers 1745.
With Chinamen and grotesques painted in sage green and
manganese purple. Grotesques, deriving from early
Roman grotto paintings, were popularised in the Italian
Renaissance by Raphael's versions and adopted as design
features by maiolica painters in Italy, Holland, France and
England.
Musée Nationale de la Céramique, Sèvres © RMN 1993

Fountain in the form of Bacchus, ht 53 cm, Orleans 1717.
An endearing piece in the sculptural tradition of the Della
Robbia and Conrade workshops, showing stylistic
affinities with both Nevers and Rouen.
*Musée Nationale de la Ceramique, Sèvres, photograph © RMN
1993*

example. The faienceries of Moustiers, established by Pierre Clerissy in the 1670s, followed
the trend for blue and white wares right up until
about 1740. The local clay was fine, hard and
pale when fired and this encouraged thinly-
potted, more refined wares. The style of painting was also more sophisticated than that of the
Rouen ware, with more attention paid to notions
of proportion and use of space. Hunting scenes
and illustrations of biblical or classical stories
were very popular, again based on contemporary engravings, and border motifs most often
derived from Chinese designs, either direct or
through the intermediary of Rouen ware. The
style Bérain, after designs by Jean Bérain a court
designer to Louis XIV, was adopted at Moustiers
in the early part of the 18th century and saw a
return to the grotesques, garlands and architectural devices of the Italian Renaissance. Joseph

Olerys, who had been in charge of the Alcora
faience factory in Spain, moved to Moustiers in
1738 and brought with him the taste for a polychrome palette and a particular liking for
orange-yellow and yellow-green tones. The
light, elegant swag and medallion style of decoration developed into a very typical Moustiers
design of fantasy figures scattered on an airy
ground of leaves and flowers.

Like Rouen, Moustiers was so successful with
its in-glaze (*grand-feu*) colours that it only dabbled in a very small way with enamel (*petit-feu*)
decoration. By contrast, Strasbourg factories
went on to adopt and perfect the technique of
enamels on tin glaze, whose palette seemed to
suit so well their Rococo tendencies. Marseilles
and many others followed suit, in an attempt to
recreate the effect of enamelled porcelain which
had become so popular in Germany and France.

Tureen in the form of a turkey, ht 49.5 cm, w 44 cm,
Strasbourg 1755.
Enamels on tin glaze.
Musee Nationale de la Ceramique, Servres, photograph
© *RMN 1993*

Strasbourg embraced the Rococo style with open arms, and its faience shows a wild, but controlled, extravagance, closely following the lead set by contemporary German porcelain designs.

Straight lines were out in favour of scallops and asymmetry. Inspiration now came directly from observation rather than second-hand from the fine arts, architecture and metalwork. Handles and knobs were in the shapes of twigs, leaves and flowers; flowers, painted from nature, adorned whole dinner services. Tureens were realistically modelled as animals, vegetables or fruit. The introduction of enamel painting to Strasbourg came with the arrival in 1749 of a group of artists who had been working at the Höchst and Meissen factories in Germany and who brought with them extensive knowledge of both chemistry and painting techniques. The refined painting is executed in a palette of colours dominated by a strong crimson. The vogue for this colour scheme had come via Meissen from Chinese *famille rose* porcelain and spread throughout France. Today it seems rather unharmonious in its combination with blue, yellow, green and brown.

The refinement, elegance and pursuit of perfection as exemplified in Strasbourg was totally in keeping with the ideals of the age. Caiger-Smith, from his contemporary viewpoint, comments on what he sees as the limitations of such preoccupations which leave no place for feeling and spontaneity:

. . . .Specialisation and perfection of technique are bound to become exclusive and ultimately to narrow the imagination through which new things are discovered . . .

. . . The ceramic work of this century, whether Italianate, chinoiserie, Germanic-

Tureen, w. 34 cm, Marseilles 1770.
With 'bouillabaisse' decoration and pomegranate handle. Enamels with predominant crimson and jade green. These colours would not have been feasible with higher temperature in-glaze pigments.
Courtesy of the Board of Trustees of the Victoria and Albert Museum

floral, rococo or neo-classical expressed the new European attitude to design as something contrived rather than evolved or discovered . . .[5]

Marseilles too adopted the Rococo style but the flavour was more rustic, more Mediterranean. As with Strasbourg ware, many of the elaborate shapes were press-moulded and the enamel (*petit-feu*) palette was used in preference to in-glaze (*grand-feu*) pigments; but the decoration had a much more homely feel with its still-life subjects of fish from the bouillabaisse and fruit and vegetables of the Midi, often an indication of the intended contents of the pot. Fishing port scenes and marine ornament were also popular.

The decline of faience as highly fashionable tableware began towards the end of the 18th century. Staffordshire whitewares (salt glaze and then creamware), cheaper, lighter and more durable for domestic use, were imported into France in large quantities after a commercial treaty in 1786 when the import duty was reduced to a nominal sum. Known in France as *faiences fines*, they were cheaper to manufacture, lighter to transport, and more durable for everyday domestic use. The luxury end of the market was taken over by the fashion for porcelain, at first brought in from Germany and later manufactured at Limoges where a natural porcelain body had been discovered. Faience proper gradually filtered down to the level of *faience populaire* where it has remained as part of the peasant pottery tradition.

Notes

[1] Lane, Arthur, *French Faience*, London (Faber and Faber, 1948)
[2] Caiger-Smith, A., *Tin-glaze Pottery in Europe and the Islamic World*, London (Faber and Faber, 1973)
[3] Ibid.
[4] Lane, A., op.cit.
[5] Caiger-Smith, A., op.cit.

General sources of reference

Giacomotti, J., *Faïences Françaises*, Fribourg (Office du Livre, 1963)
Frégnac, C., *La Faïence Européenne*, Fribourg (Office du Livre, 1976)

The Netherlands Delftware

Delftware has become synonymous with blue and white tin glaze. At the height of its golden age, which lasted approximately from the mid-17th to the mid-18th centuries, the output was the largest ever in the history of tin glaze and met a demand from all over the world. Its imitation of Chinese wares was unrivalled and as near perfect as was possible in the medium of tin-glazed earthenware.

The Dutch tin-glaze industry owed its inception to Italy but its astonishing success to the porcelain of China. By 1512 or possibly earlier, Guido Andries, the same Guido di Savino of Casteldurante mentioned by Piccolpasso, had established a pottery workshop in Antwerp. Its production consisted mainly of drug jars with simple geometric designs; tiles, good examples of which can be seen at The Vyne in Hampshire; and small altar vases. Early Antwerp pots were often illustrated in Flemish religious paintings of the 15th and 16th centuries (see opposite). Colours on the Antwerp ware were Italianate – blue, yellow, orange and green – but dominated by a very dark blue. The yellow was curiously lemony in comparison to the Italian egg yellow. Manganese was not used until much later in the Netherlands. The forms and decoration were based on Italian prototypes, chiefly of Venetian or Faentine origin, continuing such conventions as the contour panel and Italo-Moresque/Gothic-Floral motifs. 'Grotesque' style ornament was also introduced from the Urbino tradition. Another type of ware was produced in Antwerp by the rival Floris family, whose designs derived from contemporary leather and wrought iron work. Pots from Antwerp were brought back to England by wool merchants and large numbers of them have been found in excavations in the City of London.

The strategic importance of Antwerp in the history of tin glaze should not be underestimated. Sons of Guido di Savino were responsible for the spread of tin glaze to both England and Holland in the 1560s and they also made

The Adoration of the Magi, from 'The Hours of Englebert of Nassau' illuminated in Ghent by 'The Master of Mary of Burgundy', circa 1490.
Gold and tempura on vellum. The vase, dish and two-handled altar vase on the left hand side closely resemble early Antwerp ware. (There is a problem of authentication in that this miniature painting pre-dates any **known** Antwerp workshop run by Italians). The other two pieces illustrated are Hispano-Moresque.
The Bodleian Library, Oxford

tiles in Spain. The Floris family were also working in Spain round about the same time and they in turn were to influence the development of maiolica at Talavera and Triana. Other Antwerp potters settled in Portugal.

Dish with pomegranates and grapes, The Netherlands, early 17th century.
Painted in blue, yellow, rusty-orange and green with blue-dash rim.
Fitzwilliam Museum, Cambridge

The expansion of potteries in the northern Netherlands was largely the result of the political and economic upheaval during the war between Spain and the Netherlands. The Fall of Antwerp in 1585 led to a mass migration north and this undoubtedly included potters who were looking for a more favourable economic climate in which to work. Tin-glaze techniques had been introduced to Middelburg in 1564 by one of Andries' sons, but now Gouda, Rotterdam, Delft, Haarlem, Amsterdam and Frisia were all to become thriving centres, producing both pottery and tiles. The wares made in these towns from this time up until the mid-17th century are generally referred to as 'Northern Dutch Maiolica' – not only because of their Italian origin, but because of the quality of body, glaze and the manner of glazing.[1] As well as Italianate leaf patterns and geometric ornament in the Montelupo tradition, some new designs began to appear, which although probably based on contemporary Venetian fruit decoration, found a sympathetic echo in Dutch taste; cheerful pomegranates, grapes and marigolds adorn bowls and plates, reflecting the preoccupation with fruit and flowers in still-life paintings of the time; the theme of virgin and child is a simple translation of the solemn mood of Flemish religious art.

But it was, for the first time in European pottery, the discovery of Chinese porcelain that was so radically to change the course of tin-glazed earthenware in the Netherlands. Dutch explorers reached China as early as 1596 and there saw porcelain 'more exquisite than crystal'. The Dutch East India Company was founded in 1602 and began to import Chinese porcelain to Holland. In 1615 a large porcelain auction was held in Delft and the basis for Delft faience or Delftware was laid. From this time on, Chinese designs were imitated all over the Netherlands, but it was at Delft that the most refined and sophisticated wares were to be produced. The Chinese influence soon crept in. Wan-Li[2] borders of Buddhist symbols began to appear, juxtaposed with the Dutch madonnas and baskets of fruit; soon Chinese figures, landscapes and flowers were imitated, and the Chinese maze pattern formed corner motifs on tiles.

The 17th century saw a big increase in the production of tin-glazed tiles. The political annexation of the Netherlands to Spain had brought the former into contact with a much wider use of tiles. They began to be used in entrance halls, passage ways and staircases to a height of about one meter so as to protect clothing from whitewashed walls. It was a small step from there to the tiling of kitchens, fireplaces and then entire rooms. Initially, the tiles used geometric designs deriving from Hispano-Moresque and Antwerp ornament. Then the polychrome fruit and flower designs appeared. The pomegranate known in Holland as 'orange apple' and marigold were quasi-national emblems, alluding as they did to the princely House of Orange. The flower tiles are evidence of a new interest in flower painting following the discovery and importation of tulip and other bulbs to Holland. Fritillaries, lilies and tulips were copied with loving accuracy from the flower catalogues or Florilegia. Often, the flowers are in a vase, the fruit is on a fruit stand. This convention of portraying pots on pots is one which the tin-glaze tradition repeatedly adopts in its facility for quotation. Precedents are to be found in both Islamic and Turkish pottery. This type of painting remained polychrome, but for all other subjects, the Chinese palette of blue and white became almost obligatory until Rococo taste swung the preference towards manganese purple.

The Dutch Calvinists were opposed to any form of imagery in the church. Consequently art became much more secular, more democratic and reached a much wider public than ever before. Realism was the order of the day: the bourgeoisie wanted what they could see as reflections of their daily lives and immediate environment. This was the era of Vermeer and de Hooch, Cuyp and van Ruisdael, Rembrandt and Hals, of the still-life painters. The tiles with their own expressions of contemporary landscapes, seascapes, everyday scenes and flowers possessed a much more Dutch identity than the pots which went on to assimilate so totally their Chinese models as to be almost indistinguishable. The manner of the tile painting also retained a relative vigour and gestural freshness that disappeared with the striving for perfection on the pots. The Italian influence was also still apparent and artists who had travelled to Italy returned to paint Italianate landscapes, hunting and battle scenes.

Although Dutch tiles are often referred to as Delft tiles, Rotterdam was in fact the biggest producer and tile factories were operative all over the country. The export market expanded rapidly. Important commissions for tiles came from Spain, Portugal and South America at the end of the 17th century, when the Hispano-Portuguese tile industry was in decline. As has already been mentioned, Dutch tiles were sent to France for the Trianon de Porcelaine and fuelled the vogue for blue and white ceramics there. In England, William and Mary ordered tiles and pots for the decoration of Hampton Court. Architects of churches and palaces in Germany and Eastern Europe also commissioned large quantities of tiles from Holland. It was during this period that the very large tile paintings were produced. The splendid flower panels are probably the best known of these.

In the field of pottery, Delft alone went on to develop a superior glaze and finer body in emulation of the Chinese and higher artistic stan-

Porringer, The Netherlands, early 17th century.
Polychrome virgin and child (blue, yellow and green) with dark blue 'Wan-Li' border. A curious juxtaposition of intercultural iconographies.
Courtesy of the Board of Trustees of the Victoria and Albert Museum

dards pushed the decoration ever closer to the Ming models. In fact the tin-glazed ware was even referred to as 'porcelyn' because of its appearance. The very whiteness of the tin glaze must also have had considerable aesthetic appeal for the Puritans with its associations of chastity, purity, and the white ruffs and frills worn by the gentry. By the mid-17th century the quality of the tin glaze had been considerably improved and it was now applied to all surfaces of the pot (instead of just to visible ones as before). This was known as 'the white'. The Delft potters also adopted the use of a clear overglaze or *kwaart*, similar to the *coperta* used in Italy, which was flicked on to the upper and outer surfaces after painting. This created a depth and luminosity which brought Delft faience even closer to its Chinese goal. The tinting of the white glaze with minute amounts of copper or cobalt also helped to create a more 'porcellaneous' appearance. The body was developed to become finer, whiter and harder.

Tile panel, possibly an inn sign, Dutch 17th century.
With carnations, lilies and fritillaries painted in blue, yellow, rust and green.
Courtesy of the Board of Trustees of the Victoria and Albert Museum

Octagonal plaque by Frederik van Frijtom, 28cm × 28cm, dated 1662.
Painted in blue on white and intended to be framed. Pottery plaques were popular decorative items in the home.
Rijksmuseum, Amsterdam

47

Gadrooned whiteware jug, probably Delft mid-17th century. Courtesy of the Board of Trustees of the Victoria and Albert Museum

Another innovation of Delft was the use of a manganese purple outline or *trek* to give definition to the painting. This was drawn first by the artist and then the colour washes were applied within the outline, often by less skilled craftsmen. It was not long before more economical ways of repeating designs were devised and this was when pouncing or *sponsen* was introduced. Outlines were pricked through fine paper. Powdered carbon in a bag was then patted through the holes so as to transfer the pattern on to the glaze surface.

There appear to be several coincidental reasons for the growth of Delft as the main pottery centre. Geographically it was in a good position for the export of pots and the import of fine clays by means of the waterways. It was also already a thriving centre of artistic activity for painters and engravers and it was a natural step for artists to take to pottery or tile painting. Frederik van Frijtom, for example, who decorated some of the finest plaques and plates (see photograph on p.47), was not only a master potter and pottery painter, but also a highly talented and respected landscape painter in his own right. Most of the Delft potteries were destroyed by the explosion of a boat loaded with gunpowder in 1654. During the reconstruction of the city, the old breweries whose export trade had gone into decline were taken over by the expanding pottery industry. The new pottery businesses were known by the names of the breweries which is why they have such curious titles as 'The Metal Pot', 'The Greek A', 'The Peacock' and 'The Young Moor's Head'.

Many types of ware were produced in this very prolific early period. The *Wit Goet* or whitewares derived from Italian models. These simple jugs, fluted bowls, plates and other domestic pieces were often depicted in the paintings of Vermeer, de Hooch and other Delft artists of the time. They were mostly undecorated but glazed with an extra thick tin glaze known as *dubbelwit*. The gadrooned 'sunflower' bowls with their portraits of William and Mary and crudely painted borders of tulips and sunflowers are related to the whitewares and were also produced by Dutchmen at Lambeth. These and other peasant-style pots with bold, direct painting were produced throughout Holland and Caiger-Smith[3] suggests that they were used as practice pieces and kiln-fillers.

From the inspiration of Dutch painting and graphic arts came pottery painted with riverscapes, landscapes, rural life, interiors – also plaques with ceramic frames destined for the living room. Biblical scenes were popular as were portraits of scientists, theologians and historians.

The *Wapengoet* fulfilled a demand from the upper classes for heraldic ware featuring family coats of arms. Sets of dinner plates were also inscribed with Dutch rhymes – one couplet on each plate. This tradition became very popular in England (e.g. 'merryman' plates). *Straets Goet* were imitations of Italian designs brought in via the Straits of Gibraltar. From about 1675, the *Kaapsche Schotel* (plates from the Cape) began to be produced. These were finely executed imitations of Chinese Ming imports, usually featuring

Tulip vase, ht 175 cm, Delft circa 1720.
Painted in blue and white with manganese 'trek' (outline).
The decoration shows a mixed pedigree of Rouen
lambrequins, Dutch landscapes (not visible here) and
oriental motifs.
Musée du Louvre, photograph © RMN 1993

a central polygonal medal and subdivided border.

The 18th century saw a wealth of new ingredients absorbed into the Dutch Delftware repertoire: The Ch'ing dynasty in China provided a whole new range of ornament and brought the polychrome palette back into fashion; the *famille verte* inspired the use of enamels and gilding; teapots with dark coloured glazes imitated Chinese lacquer ware; Chinese and Italian influences reached a kind of fusion. Fresh material came from Japanese Imari designs. But Europe too provided new impetus: the Baroque movement inevitably made its mark – most evident in complex forms such as the tulip vases (see photograph on p.49). Rouen in its turn also cross-fertilised Delftware and inspired a greater variety of shapes, objects and decorative motifs.

Plate, diam 27 cm, Delft probably 19th century.
This pattern of Japanese derivation became a standard design in the 18th century Dutch repertoire. Early examples were polychrome, but as volume and speed of production increased in the 19th century, a simpler, standardised blue and white version such as this one was produced using transfers and painting.
Collection of Carew Treffgarne. Photograph by Douglas Cape.

After about 1750, the high artistic standards and perfection of workmanship which had characterised Dutch Delftware for the past century began to tail off. Rococo-style trinkets, toys and butter dishes were produced in an effort to stem the twin tides of German porcelain and English creamware which were beginning to flood the European market. In a sense, the entrepreneurial nature of the Dutch Delftware industry also sowed the seeds of its own destruction. It became so adept at imitating, so concerned with profit, that imagination, spontaneity and flexibility were gradually eased out of the process. It had however been extraordinarily successful in its ability to reflect the taste of the day for perfect craftsmanship and elegance. The business-like production of traditional-style delftware on a large scale has been continued since that time by such factories as Tichelaars at Makkum and De Porceleyne Fles at Delft.

Notes

[1] 'Maiolica' is a term often used by ceramic historians to distinguish cruder Italianate wares from the later, more refined European 'faience'. With maiolica, as with its Italian prototypes, tin glaze was used only on the visible surfaces; underneaths and insides were glazed with the cheaper transparent lead glaze. These wares are considered crude in comparison to the materials and techniques that went into the development of Delftware and other so-called faience of the 17th and 18th centuries – products more related to porcelain, oriental and European, than to Italian maiolica. In fact, this sort of terminology is often confusing and could well be dispensed with altogether!

[2] Emperor of the Ming dynasty 1573–1619

[3] cf. Caiger-Smith, A., *Tin-glaze Pottery in Europe and the Islamic World*, London (Faber and Faber, 1973)

Other Sources of Reference for this Chapter are:

De Jonge, C., *Delft Ceramics*, London (Pall Mall Press, 1970)

Berendsen, A., *Tiles*, London (Faber and Faber, 1967)

Fourest, H.-P., *Delftware*, London (Thames and Hudson, 1980)

English Delftware

Although tin-glazed ware in England started out, as in so many other countries, in the Italianate mode, and emanated from Antwerp, it soon acquired a very different character from that of its European counterparts. In parallel with the qualities of the slipware made by Thomas Toft and his contemporaries, there is a relaxed tone and a sprightliness which is preserved throughout the history of English delftware; the overriding mood is provincial and naive rather than urbane and sophisticated. The variety of expression is prodigious. Tin-glazed ware was at first referred to in England as 'galleyware'.[1] It wasn't until the 18th century, when Dutch Delftware became so well-known, that 'delftware' became the generic term for tin-glazed earthenware in England.

It seems that tin-glazed wares may have been made in England even before the arrival of the Antwerp potters. A group of jugs based on Rhenish stoneware shapes, with round bellies and straight necks have been dated back to about 1550. These are called 'Malling jugs' from examples found at West Malling church in Kent although their place of manufacture is uncertain and there is speculation that they may have come from the Low Countries. The glazes are either plain coloured or mottled, probably in imitation of Rhenish salt glaze (tigerware). Some of them were silver-mounted. They are quite special pieces and appear to be isolated examples in the history of tin glaze. They bear no obvious relation to the subsequent development of delftware in England, which began independently.

Religious persecution by the Spanish in Flanders was responsible for the emigration of Antwerp potters to other countries in the 1560s.

Protestant Holland and England must have been attractive havens to the Huguenot refugees. Among those to flee were Jasper Andries (a son of Guido Andries) and Jacob Jansen, who first came to Norwich in 1567, where they made paving tiles and apothecary vessels.

In 1570, Andries and Jansen sent a petition to Queen Elizabeth requesting the sole right to practice 'galleypotting' in London and shortly afterwards Jansen had set up a workshop in Aldgate along with six other Flemish potters. In the early 1600s tin-glaze potters moved first to Southwark and then after the Restoration in 1661 expanded to Lambeth. Outside London, the two main delftware centres in the British Isles were Bristol, set up by potters from Southwark in the 1650s and Liverpool, established in 1712. Other important factories were at Glasgow and Dublin. All of these places were thriving ports and were therefore not only well-placed for exporting pots and importing supplies but also more susceptible to foreign influences.[2]

French faience reached the very peak of fashionability throughout Europe and satisfied a real need among the aristocracy for large quantities of grand tableware. Dutch delftware was of the highest technical standards and came very close to Chinese originals. Its mass marketing was carried out by astute businessmen who also organised production. English delftware remained on a much more humble level. Its patronage consisted mostly of middle-class merchant families and country gentry; the status of the potter was more lowly than that of his European counterparts; the wares produced were in comparison simpler in both intent and execution.

Technically too, English delftware did not entertain the complexities of some of the Continental methods. The use of a transparent overglaze similar to the Dutch *kwaart* or the Italian *coperta* was only dabbled with briefly. Enamels, or *petit-feu* pigments, which swept the Continent in the 18th century were used only for a short period at Liverpool. The British Isles were fortunate to have good sources of high-lime earthenware clays (gault clays) which were eminently suitable to take a tin glaze, firing to a pale buff colour and with a high shrinkage so as to eliminate the crazing which would occur on most local soft red clays. Clay from East Anglia was used first in Norwich and then shipped to both London and Holland. In 1681 a new source of gault clay was opened up near the Medway river in Aylsford, Kent and this was subsequently used by the London workshops.

Bristol, Liverpool, Glasgow and Dublin all brought in clay from Carrickfergus on the Belfast Lough to mix with local clays. Cornwall was the main supplier of tin all over the Continent. It was expensive abroad but plentiful in England and would explain the high opacity and often fatty quality of the English glazes.

The early wares produced at Aldgate are mostly indistinguishable from those made in Antwerp and are often collectively attributed and referred to as 'Anglo-Netherlandish'. These include altar vases (see illustration on p. 44), tiles and apothecary jars in Italianate colours and designs. London production of attractively simple albarello drug jars with banding, chevrons and various geometric motifs continued up until the end of the 17th century.

The earliest known dated piece of English delftware is a dish, now in the Museum of London. The design consists of a central scene of a city with castellated towers, surrounded by an inscription, 'THE ROSE IS RED THE LEAVES ARE GRENE GOD SAVE ELIZABETH OUR QUEENE' and bordered with Antwerpesque motifs. It has a rim with blue dashes. The date in

Charger, diam. 50.8 cm, Southwark 1659.
Painted in Italianate (Montelupo) palette of blue, green, yellow and rusty-orange. The central picture illustrates the story of the Prodigal Son and shows the influence of Dutch landscape painting. The border is an anglicised interpretation of Italian Renaissance grotesques.
Reproduced by courtesy of the Trustees of the British Museum

Albarello, ht 12.4 cm, Southwark early 17th century.
Painted in blue and orange-yellow.
Museum of London

Charger, diam. 33.4 cm, blue and orange painting, probably London circa 1660.
Bristol Museums and Art Gallery

Adam and Eve charger, diam. 40.6 cm. London circa 1660–75. Decorated in yellow, manganese, green and blue with blue-dash border.
Ashmolean Museum, Oxford

the centre of the design is 1600. This appears to be a prototype of the 'blue-dash charger', one of the most decorative and delightful of all English wares, produced by London and Bristol workshops until the early 18th century. As they were made purely for decorative purposes, to grace side table or wall, many of them have survived in excellent condition. In the maiolica pictorial tradition, they were decorated in a broadly Italianate polychrome palette and most often glazed underneath with a clear lead glaze. The charger became a vehicle for several distinctive types of design. The earlier pieces bear witness to the pervasive mood of Dutch/Italian styles. Some of these have central pictorial scenes – rural, domestic, architectural, marine, biblical, naive translations of Dutch genre painting. Rims are articulated with Italianate borders of floral motifs, grotesques, arabesques and the like. Some are purely geometric in design and have a tremendous calligraphic verve. Others continue the early North Netherlandish/Venetian designs of luscious pomegranates, grapes and leaves.

A much more English flavour emerges in the tulip, Adam and Eve and portrait chargers. The tulip designs – their formal qualities sometimes simplified almost to abstraction – represent for me English delftware at its most expressive and

free; the use of space is extraordinarily bold for the period and appears without precedent in the maiolica tradition. However, contemporary Isnik dishes also show similar arrangements of flowers springing from one point on the circumference or from a vase and may well have been in the consciousness of the Flemish potters working in England.[3] Adam and Eve was a very popular decoration. The subject was inspired by but not slavishly copied from biblical engravings and the very charm of this decoration lies in the spirited, freehand interpretation, although later the style of painting tended to degenerate into sheer sloppiness.

Royal portraits also came to be very closely associated with English delftware and chargers in particular. These began to appear with Charles I[4] and continued through the reigns of Charles II, James II, William and Mary, Queen Anne and Georges I and II. They commonly show the monarch either in an architectural setting, amongst trees or seated on a horse. Some of the later portraits show just the head and shoulders. Mugs featuring Charles II with the date of his coronation in 1661 must be among the earliest examples of royal souvenir pottery (see photographs on p. 54).

Quite another strain of English tin glaze was to develop from a workshop set up at Pickleherring

William and Mary plate, diam. approx 20 cm, greenish glaze with blue and yellow painting, probably Lambeth 1691.
Economical and effective use of brushwork. Almost a caricature, as little attempt is made at accurate portraiture.
Ashmolean Museum, Oxford

Caudle cup, ht 7.3 cm. Southwark 1661.
Decorated in blue, manganese, yellow and ochre.
Museum of London

Tulip charger, diam. 32.2 cm, probably London, 1676.
This decorative theme was interpreted in many different ways, but always made bold use of composition in relation to form. These designs are far removed from mere pictorial illusionism.
Fitzwilliam Museum, Cambridge

54

Quay, Southwark, in 1612 by one Christian Wilhelm. Also from the Low Countries, he was the first important producer of tin-glazed ware and the first to introduce oriental influences.[5] As well as being a galleypotter, he was also a manufacturer of smalt (cobalt pigment), and was therefore in an advantageous position to exploit the oriental palette of blue and white. The 'bird on a rock' pattern, with attendant ferns, flowers, insects and clouds, is very typical of the Pickleherring pottery. Although inspired by Ming designs, the all-over distribution of the motifs is evocative of Elizabethan embroidery and tapestry work.[6] Wares made were domestic and included mugs, posset pots,[7] wine bottles and dishes. The posset pot, albeit utilitarian, was seen as a more special piece and gave scope for ornamental indulgence on handles and lid. Inscriptions and dates also feature on the pots and the commemorative nature of English delftware continued to be prominent throughout its production.[8] The 'bird on a rock' design was later superseded in popularity by the enduring

Posset pot, ht 34.7 cm. Lambeth or Bristol, dated 1685 (on pot) and 1686 (on stand).
An elaborate example of the posset pot, illustrating its function as a ceremonial piece. The 'Chinese figures in a landscape' was one of the most recurrent decorative themes of English delftware.
Fitzwilliam Museum, Cambridge

Betrothal or wedding mug, Southwark (Pickleherring), 1631–2. Inscribed 'William and Elizabeth'. 'Bird on a rock' design painted in blue on white.
Courtesy of the Board of Trustees of the Victoria and Albert Museum

'Chinaman in a landscape' theme. Although the Chinese influence was strong in both Dutch and English wares, its effects in the two countries were quite different. Whereas the Dutch designs were faithful reproductions, the English interpretations were looser, more fanciful versions filtered through European eyes and best described by the term 'Chinoiserie'. In this early period there were also English imitations of the *bleu de Nevers* technique, sometimes simply in the form of crude white blotches on a blue ground (see photograph on p. 56).

The tin-glaze tradition of whitewares with little or no pigment decoration was exemplified by the production in London of some of the most charmingly restrained pieces. Pigment decoration when it occurs is minimal and shows little trace of Italian or Chinese influence. The walls of some shapes e.g. mugs and posset pots have obviously been modelled by the potter's finger while the clay was still wet into soft, regular bumps. Forms included salts, candlesticks, moulded dishes, fuddling cups,[9] puzzle jugs, flower vases with multiple spouts, and most notably bellarmine-shaped wine bottles. Decoration on the bottles was restricted to identification

Posset pot, London 17th century.
A humble example in comparison with the posset pot on p. 55.
Courtesy of the Board of Trustees of the Victoria and Albert Museum

Fluted bowl, diam. 22 cm, white glaze blotches on dark blue tin glaze, probably London circa 1700.
A crude derivation of the *bleu de Nevers* technique.
Bristol Museums and Art Gallery

Barber's bowl, diam. 30.5 cm, probably London circa 1725.
Painted in blue. Has all the equipment not only of a barber but of a barber-surgeon.
Museum of London

Wine bottle, ht 18.7 cm, blue painting on a pinkish glaze, Southwark 1640.
Museum of London

of contents[10] and a calligraphic flourish; the rich mutton-fat quality of the glaze is therefore shown to maximum advantage. The use of pottery wine bottles died out in the 1670s when glass bottles were introduced.

Apothecary wares, now mainly blue and white, continued to be made in addition to new items such as the barber's bowl, pill slabs, bleeding bowls and porringers. English delftware never went in for ostentation in the way that the Continental factories did. The punchbowl came to replace the posset pot towards the end of the 17th century as a quasi-ceremonial centrepiece for the table and was the nearest English equivalent to the Continental tureen. Some pieces, such as the splendid ship bowls and the eccentric cat jugs, were peculiar to English delftware. Others were English versions of items already established in the tin-glaze repertoire: book handwarmers, shoes,[11] flower bricks, wall pockets, inkstands and figurines.

In the 17th century, there were inevitable parallels with Dutch wares, particularly in view of the fact that for a while the two countries had the same rulers, William and Mary. Similarities are to be found in the scalloped 'sunflower' dishes, the 'merryman' plates with their witty inscriptions, the use of a turquoise-tinted glaze and the dark manganese or cobalt *trek* line.

England was not immune to the fashions of the 18th century and several developments are perceptible. Teapots, coffee pots and other genteel tablewares took over from the cruder utilitarian wares of the 17th century. The chinoiserie style, although more sophisticated, still retained a freshness and spontaneity lacking in the Continental wares with their streamlined methods of production. In accordance with Continental taste, the polychrome palette was back, but, following the examples of Rouen and Delft, the Italianate palette of blue, yellow, orange, bright green was now superseded by a combination of blue, sage green (antimony and cobalt) and brick red (haematite or red ochre). Later the Rococo vogue gave rise to a proliferation of coloured powdered grounds, and a preference for manganese pinks and liverish reds. The *bianco sopra bianco* technique was also popular for a while. In the mid-18th century, the paintings of Gainsborough and his contemporaries stimulated a wave of pottery decorated with aristocratic figures in an English landscape.

Flower brick, ht 8 cm, bluish glaze with blue painting, probably Bristol circa 1745–60.
The 'Figures in an English Landscape' theme is juxtaposed with Chinese motifs.
Ashmolean Museum, Oxford

Coffee pot, ht 19.1 cm, painted in blue, yellow, iron-red and green, probably Lambeth, dated 1705.
Ashmolean Museum, Oxford

Porcelain decoration was responsible for the return of floral ornament during the same period and the Fazackerley designs have a distinctive, chintzy, very English character. They were almost exclusively made in Liverpool which became the most fashionable and technically advanced producer of delftware in the 18th century. The ship bowls, made at both Liverpool and Bristol and commissioned by captains of trading ships, are a testimony to the English love of the sea. More in the line of peasant pottery were the popular plates decorated in a very fluid manner with animals and birds of farmyard and estate. The most common subjects were the rooster and the peacock, often against a background of manganese-sponged trees.

The Industrial Revolution and the rise of the Staffordshire potteries between them spelt the end of delftware in England. White earthenware clays were cheap and plentiful. Decoration, most often by now in transfer form, could be applied direct to the bisqued surface and glazed with a transparent glaze and the end product was more durable than the soft-bodied, thickly-glazed delftware. Increasingly mechanised and industrial methods of manufacture from the end of the 18th century also meant that the peasant pottery tradition, where designs and techniques were handed down from father to son and where tin-glazed wares might have survived, was now phased out (with the exception of some country workshops making utilitarian terracotta or lead-glazed items). Tin-glazed earthenware virtually died out until its reappearance as a form of art pottery in the late 19th century.

Ship bowl, diam. 27 cm, ht 11.1 cm, probably Liverpool 1747. Painted in blue with touches of red and yellow, on off-white glaze. These punch bowls were made to order for ships calling at the ports of Liverpool or Bristol. Records show that the Lively was in the habit of carrying earthenware among her cargo, and was therefore likely to have had direct contact with the delftware factories.
Bristol Museums and Art Gallery

Notes

1 Possibly from the Dutch word *glei* meaning porcelain clay or in reference to the import of tin-glazed wares in galleys, *cf.* Britton F., *English Delftware in the Bristol Collection*, London (Sotheby Publications, 1982)

2 Pointed out by Emmanuel Cooper in his *History of World Pottery*, London (Batsford, 1981)

3 Venetian potteries made copies of Isnik designs in maiolica so Isnik pots were obviously admired and brought over to Europe in the 16th century. There are also at least four pieces of Isnik (in the Victoria and Albert Museum and in the British Museum) with English 16th century silver mounts.

4 Described by Rubens as 'the greatest amateur of painting among the princes of the world'. This great patron of the arts brought many craftsmen and artists to London, including Van Dyck who was to become a major influence on English portrait painting.

5 There is some doubt as to whether this influence was first- or second-hand i.e. direct from Chinese porcelain or via Dutch delftware – opinion now seems to favour the first theory *cf.* Britton, F., op.cit.

6 An interesting comment of Alan Caiger-Smith's in his *Tin-glaze Pottery in Europe and the Islamic World*, London (Faber and Faber, 1973)

7 Posset was a sweet dessert drink made of wine, eggs, cream and honey. It was drunk through the spout of the posset pot.

8 A frequent device employed three initials in triangular arrangement and commemorated a betrothal or marriage – the two lower initials representing the two Christian names, the middle, higher one, the family name.

9 From the old English word 'fuddle' ‹=› to confuse. An ale mug joined in multiples of three, four or five with connecting holes. Along with the puzzle jug, a joke drinking vessel used in taverns.

10 The most common wines were claret, 'whit' (white) and 'sack' (export sherry).

11 In France used for champagne, here probably as flower vases or ornaments.

In addition to the above-mentioned publications by Frank Britton and Alan Caiger-Smith, the chief sources of reference for this chapter are:

Britton, F., *London Delftware*, London (Jonathan Horne, 1987)

Garner, F.H. and Archer, Michael, *English Delftware*, London (Faber and Faber, 1972)

Ray, Anthony, *English Delftware in the Robert Hall Warren Collection*, Ashmolean Museum, Oxford, London (Faber and Faber, 1968)

Lipski, L. & M. Archer, *Dated English Delftware*, London (Sotheby's, 1984)

Plate, diam 17.6 cm, probably Bristol circa 1720
Decorated in blue, red and yellow with manganese-sponged trees.
Bristol Museums and Art Gallery

Cross-Fertilisations

The development
of tin glaze in other countries

Previous chapters have discussed continuous developments in France, Holland and England through to the end of the 18th century when tin-glaze production as a 'high' art form virtually ceased. Although the scope of this book does not permit extensive study of the subject, mention must now be made of other areas of development during this period. In this golden age, before competition from white earthenware and porcelain became too strong, maiolica spread like wildfire throughout Europe. Initially the technical know how and the aesthetic code came either directly or indirectly from Italy; then the pressures of Baroque and Rococo movements were brought to bear; each country responded in a different way to these influences and went on to develop its own very distinct character. Countries such as Spain and Italy which had earlier experienced powerful creative expressions in the medium, were also during this time subject to the impact of new and foreign influences.

Spain was the first country to experience the influence of Italian Renaissance maiolica (having itself previously been an inspiration to Italy). From before 1500, the Italian ceramicist Nicoluso Pisano was working in Triana, making architectural tiles and reliefs in Faentine style – among them the Visitation panel in the Alcazar, Seville and the doorway of the Convent of Santa Paula in Triana. Italian and Flemish potters were employed in similar architectural projects throughout the 16th century. In the latter half of this century, the impact of *istoriato* began to be felt and centres such as Talavera, Triana, Toledo and Puente del Arzobispo all responded to this new stimulus. A shortage of silver in Spain also meant an increased demand for pottery as table-ware. Talavera, the most prolific producer, used a brilliant Italianate palette to create a wide variety of pictorial designs, some of the most popular being bullfight or hunting scenes. Many designs however, were relatively unaffected by Italian influences and retained a distinctive Spanish flavour. In the 18th century the pottery centre of Alcora brought artists from Moustiers and Marseilles to teach Spaniards the art of decorating in the accepted mode of the day. Thus chinoiserie, arabesques, Rococo floral sprays and such-like were introduced to Spanish eyes.

Plate of the type known as 'platos de pino', diam. 38.3 cm, Puente del Arzobispo. early 19th century.
Painted in green, yellow and orange and outlined in manganese.
Fitzwilliam Museum, Cambridge

Dish painted in dark blue, Castile (probably Puente del Arzobispo), late 16th or early 17th century.
Robust decoration and a good example of a very large group of pieces in this style. According to Anthony Ray, the group is often called the mariposa *(butterfly) series on account of the border seen on the dish, but there are other types of border.*
Reproduced by Courtesy of the Trustees of the British Museum

Italy, although it no longer had a leading role in European tin glaze, went on to a more relaxed and varied production of maiolica which followed the mood of the Faenza whitewares with their minimal decoration. Rococo Italy followed the suit of France and Germany and Holland in their fairly wholesale adoption of the *petit-feu* technique. Tin-glazed earthenware continued to thrive in both Italy and Spain as part of a strong peasant pottery tradition and this will be discussed later.

Portugal, acquainted with tin glaze since Moorish times, was settled by Flemish potters in the 1560s and imported quantities of Dutch tiles in the 17th century. It was also, through its sea-trading activities in the Far East, very susceptible to the influence of Chinese porcelain and readily adopted the blue and white palette. Portugal's most important tin-glaze heritage lies in its

Dish, diam 32.5 cm, Montelupo 'compendario' style, circa 1625.
Painted in grey-blue, yellow, orange, dark manganese purple and copper green.
Courtesy of the Board of Trustees of the Victoria and Albert Museum

Tile panel, painted in green, yellow, blue and manganese brown, Portuguese (Pombaline style), circa 1760–1780. Museu da Cidade, Lisbon. By kind permission of PORTUGAL 600.
Photograph by Lucinda Symons

splendid tradition of tiles, known as *azulejos*; these were made from the 16th century onwards and constituted an integral part of religious and domestic architecture.

Germany was already familiar with tin-glaze techniques in the early 1500s, when tin glazes were used with coloured glazes on relief-moulded wares. The technique was also adopted by the stove-tile makers (Hafners) and some rather bizarre 'owl' jugs (ancient precursors of the Martin brothers' ware?) were made in the mid-16th century. However, the main wave of tin-glaze production was to come much later in the 17th century, following the establishment at Hanau in 1661 of a tin-glaze pottery by a group of Dutch religious refugees. From then on, the Oriental/Delft style was to dominate the

course of German faience until well into the 18th century. Frankfurt in particular produced very high quality wares and also used the *kwaart* overglaze technique.[1] At Nuremberg and Augsburg, painters of the German Baroque were brought in to decorate 'Hausmaler' jugs in enamels. In the 18th century the main influence on faience in Germany came from porcelain forms and decoration, but there were also cross-pollinations back from Rouen and Strasbourg.

Stove tile, 31.9cm × 22.5cm, probably Cologne 1572 or later. Moulded in relief with a scene from the Parable of the Prodigal Son. White tin glaze and coloured transparent glazes (green, blue, yellow, brown, purple).
Reproduced by permission of the Trustees of the Wallace Collection

Höchst produced a large number of faience animals, either as vessels or as models and these were much imitated at Strasbourg and Delft. German faience too fell victim to English creamware. Although tin glaze continued to be made in some areas it was not as popular as stoneware, whose manufacture was facilitated by plentiful supplies of cheap coal. Scandinavia's proximity to Germany accounted for the spread of the faience industry to Schleswig-Holstein, Sweden, Denmark and Norway in the 18th century.

The tin-glaze traditions of Switzerland, Bohemia, Moravia, Slovakia and Hungary most probably also owed their origins to Italy. Anabaptists ('New Christians') fleeing religious persecution in Italy in the 16th century settled in Winterthur, Switzerland and, in addition to the manufacture of stove tiles, brought with them a very particular kind of pottery. Deriving in concept from the *bianchi di Faenza*, it was simply made with sparse, restrained but quite charming decoration. As their religious convictions forbade any representations of human or animal figures, fruit and flower motifs were the main

Haban plate of Renaissance form, diam. 27 cm, painted in blue, orange and green with manganese outline, Sobotist region, 1674.
Fitzwilliam Museum, Cambridge

type of ornament used, often in combination with coats of arms and commemorative inscriptions. This type of decoration was also carried over to Eastern Europe by descendants of the Anabaptists, known as 'Habaner', and there it gradually became fused with indigenous folk art. The tin-glaze tradition has remained strong throughout Czechoslovakia and Hungary since that time.

Puebla tiles, painted in blue, Mexico 17th century.
Courtesy of the Board of Trustees of the Victoria and Albert Museum

In the New World, tin glaze took root in Mexico following the arrival of Spanish craftsmen after the Conquest in the 16th century. Of the Mahgreb, only Morocco remained with a consistent tradition of tin glaze – its decoration of dense geometric pattern quite separate from the development of other Islamic tin-glaze designs.

Note

[1] There is now, however, much debate among historians as to whether the so-called Frankfurt ware was made in Frankfurt or in Delft.

Storage jar from Meknes, Morocco, 18th century.
Painted in black, blue, green and yellow.
The Oriental Museum, Durham University

The Artist's Medium

New Visions in the 19th and 20th Centuries

Tin-glaze pottery's golden age of innovation, development, refinement and commercial success throughout Europe lasted from the 15th to the start of the 19th century. Since the demise of the golden age, the application of tin glaze seems to fall roughly into two categories: on the one hand, a vigorous peasant pottery tradition where the emphasis is on perpetuating a vernacular style and meeting local needs; on the other, the use of tin glaze as medium of the individual artist, closely linked to movements in the fine and applied arts and uncompromised by concerns of mass production and profitability. This new input of creative energies was to come chiefly from outside the world of ceramics, from architecture, sculpture and especially from painting. The appearance of the Artist-Potter at the end of the 19th century was partly a reaction to the inadequacies of industrial pottery, where ever greater mechanical routine and subdivision of labour left no room for personal creativity.

In England, William Morris was the first artist[1] to react to what Nikolaus Pevsner (in *Pioneers of Modern Design*) describes as the 'philistinism and squalor' of mass-produced art. Rejecting the Industrial Age as dehumanising, his socialistic crusade aimed to reunite art with the people and revive the status of handmade crafts. The Arts and Crafts movement, embodying Morris's ideas, brought with it a revival of artistic designer-craftsmanship and a new interest in applied arts for the home. William de Morgan was one of the young artists of the Arts and Crafts movement. He designed stained glass, tiles and furniture panels for Morris's firm, before setting up his own workshop. Heavily influenced by Islamic and Hispano-Moresque

ware, he revived the art of reduced-pigment lustres on tin glaze to an extraordinarily high standard and created a subtle palette ranging from deep red and pink to yellow and grey. He also developed a range of 'Persian' coloured alkaline glazes. In their inherent historicism, with constant reference to Middle Eastern and Italian sources, de Morgan's designs were very much of their Victorian time; visually too, they had much in common with the stylised, carefully organised ornament of Morris. From the early 1870s until about 1905, he was designing and producing tiles and pots. Although he himself carried out extensive research into glazes,

William De Morgan, dish diam. 37 cm, 1880s.
Painted in ruby and yellow lustres on tin glaze.
Courtesy of the Board of Trustees of the Victoria and Albert Museum

pigments and lustres, in other respects he was primarily a designer, buying in tile blanks and hollow ware for decoration and employing skilled decorators to execute his designs.

The design-orientated Wiener Werkstätte founded in Vienna in 1903 by Josef Hoffmann and Koloman Moser, was based on notions clearly deriving from the ideas of Ruskin and Morris. It too abhorred the shoddiness of industrial goods, wanted to bridge the gap between art and craftsmanship and create a unified vision of architecture and the applied arts. Its outlook however contained the seeds of an aesthetic framework very different from that of the backward-looking Arts and Crafts and it ultimately led to the genesis of the Modern movement and its incarnation in the Bauhaus. The Wiener Werkstätte's search for a contemporary idiom was expressed in a philosophy of truth to materials, a mistrust of historicism and a basic acceptance of the Machine Age.

Lotte Calm-Wierink, group produced at the Wiener Werkstätte, circa 1918–25.
Reproduced by permission of Dr W. Neuwirth.

Early ceramics of the Wiener Werkstätte took the form of close liaisons between artist-designers and factories in the production of austere functional shapes, either plain or with geometric decoration. In 1906 the Wiener Keramik was founded by Michael Powolny and Bertold Löffler. Its products were commissioned and marketed by the Wiener Werkstätte and were employed on grand projects such as the making of tiles for the Palais Stoclet in Brussels. A general trend away from the early austerity began to emerge; there was a resurgence of historical ornamentalism and a return to traditional techniques such as tin-glazed earthenware. Artefacts produced included fireplaces and tiled stoves, candelabras, tea and coffee sets, strawberry services and innumerable vases, but, under Powolny's lead, there was a particular revival of interest in figure modelling[2] combined with maiolica painting in Della Robbia tradition. The full impact of this trend was not felt until after 1917, when the Wiener Werkstätte began to produce its own ceramics, and it lasted until the late 1920s. This new Viennese eclecticism was exemplified in the work of such artists as Robert Obsieger, Dagobert Peche, Susi Singer, Margrit Kovacs, Lotte Calm-Wierink and Gudrun Baudisch, all of whom had trained under Powolny at the Kunstgewerbeschule. The overall effect of much of this work is far removed from the functional simplicity of the early Wiener Werkstätte – lively, decorative and charmingly frivolous at its best, verging on kitsch at its worst – and best described as 'Kleinkunst' (literally 'little art').

France was the cradle of the artist-potter and examples of fruitful collaboration between painter and potter in France go back as far as the mid-19th century. Probably the first artist-potter in the modern sense, working in a completely autonomous way, was Théodore Deck who set himself up in Paris in 1856 to produce decorative earthenware. As well as researching into Persian and Turkish glaze techniques and writing a book on faience, he called on the skills of artists such as Félix Bracquemond and Eléanore Escallier to produce decorated *faience fine* (white earthenware with clear glaze). A new-found freedom from symmetry in the designs demonstrates the powerful influence of *japonisme* which swept through artistic circles in the wake of the Paris Exhibitions, where Japanese pottery had been on show for the first time in France. In the 1880s, Emile Gallé of the Art Nouveau Ecole de Nancy

Albarello-shaped slipcast vase, ht 20 cm, by Phyllis Keyes, painting by Duncan Grant, 1930s.
The goldfish was one of Grant's favourite themes.
Courtesy of Crafts Council and David Cripps

made some tin-glazed, enamelled pieces of oriental inspiration and Paul Gauguin turned his hand to ceramics (stoneware) in Ernest Chaplet's studio.

However, it was André Metthey's adventurous experiment with Fauve painters in the early years of this century that contributed so much to the re-instatement of tin glaze as a painter's medium.[3] The painterly, expressive, approach to decoration on these pieces was, in both spirit and content, a precursor of modern idioms. When other potters were still obsessed with Far Eastern high-temperature glaze techniques, Metthey was alone in championing the cause of faience as an instrument in the creative renewal of ceramic decoration; he challenged contemporary perceptions of faience as ordinary (*commune*), maintaining that a soft-fired body was not *per se* an indication of inferior ceramic quality. A self-taught potter, inspired whilst in the army by Garnier's *Traité de Céramique*, Metthey set up his studio in Asnières (near Paris) in 1903. After some early experiments with stoneware he became very attracted to the tradition of French faience. He prepared his own clay and tin glaze. The clay body was made from a mixture of *terre verte* (high iron, fusible clay) from Fresne, *marne* (high-lime marl) from Meudon and sand from Fontenay-les-Roses. He stressed the importance of using local materials to retain vernacular qualities which had become lost with industrialised methods of production. Metthey's studio was a meeting place for various artists of the Ecole de Paris as well as the influential art dealer Ambroise Vollard. The potter's awareness of colour must have been heightened by his constant contact with painters who used colour in such a bold, primitivist way, and he prepared a range of brilliant pigments for use on tin glaze. Maybe lacking in confidence to paint himself, he invited his artist friends to exercise their talents on his pots. The list of participants is long and star-studded – Auguste Renoir, Odilon Redon, Georges Rouault, Edouard Vuillard, Pierre Bonnard, Maurice Denis, Van Dongen, André Derain, Maurice de Vlaminck, Henri Matisse, Pierre Laprade, Jean de Puy, Luce, Othon Friesz, the sculptor Aristide Maillol and Georgette Agutte. At the Salon d'Automne in 1907, one hundred of these painted tin-glazed pieces were shown. This collaborative effort was alas short-lived, with the exception of Rouault

Maurice de Vlaminck and André Metthey, vase, ht 54 cm, 1907–9.
Musée d'art moderne de la Ville de Paris © SPADEM, 1993

who continued working with Metthey for the next four years and supplied orders passed on by Vollard. The artists were attracted to the transformation and permanence of fired ceramic pigments; they also saw in the project the opportunity to enlarge their decorative and visual language, to dispense totally with 'space box' perspectival illusion in the animation of three-dimensional surfaces. It is possible that in the end the lack of technical knowledge and the challenge of dealing with changing tonal values from raw to fired colour proved too much for the artists. In any case, the legacy was inspirational and paved the way for many like-minded partnerships.

Roger Fry had much admired the faience painting of Vlaminck and had included some in his Post-Impressionist Exhibition in London in 1912. The Omega Workshops, which in its ceramics perpetuated much of the spirit of the Metthey-Fauve enterprise, was founded by Fry in 1913 and constituted an extraordinary chapter in the history of British art and craft. Based on Continental models of the Wiener Werkstätte and couturier Poiret's Studio Martine,[4] the aim was to employ artists to work directly on the production of a completely new look for the applied arts in the service of the home. Like Morris, Fry too had been disillusioned with the commercial exploitation of pottery claiming that 'the machine substitutes an ideal exactitude for a felt approximation. . . . Wherever the machine enters, the nervous tremor of the creator disappears'. Unlike Morris, there was no overt moralistic or socialistic message, but rather a more general aesthetic-based striving to renew spontaneity and creative energy in the applied arts through the direct intervention of the artist. Ostentation, fussiness and historical pastiche were considered decadent and alienating. In the Fauves' intuitive sense of colour and pattern, Fry had shrewdly envisaged a wider impact in the field of the applied arts. The exhilarating, life-enhancing nature of bright colour and pattern was seen as a corrective to the dinginess of the British home interior and one which would elicit a pleasurable response. Fry's choice for the majority of Omega ceramics, of maiolica, with its Mediterranean colour associations, was therefore a deliberate one. Pottery was seen as a craft which eminently lends itself to communication, readily evocative of response on many levels. Fry made a point of learning to throw pots himself and he also studied glaze technology at Camberwell for a time. He made many of the Omega pots, some glazed in plain tin glaze, others decorated in maiolica pigments by Vanessa Bell and Duncan Grant. The Workshops were closed in 1919 due to a variety of factors – the war, inefficient administration and high cost of maintaining the artists. Although the products had sold well to one strata of society – the artistic intelligentsia and the 'smart motorcar set ladies', Omega had failed in its efforts to reach a wider public. Its fresh and lively spirit prevailed however in the continuing decorative work of Grant and Bell (working with potters Phyllis Keyes and Quentin Bell) up until the 1940s (see photograph on p.67). As well as decorating tin-glazed studio pottery, the two artists also did some designing for industrial ceramics. Of Omega pottery, Quentin Bell wrote:

It is a prototype of the ceramics of our century. From it a generation has learned to avoid fussiness and indecision and yet it also has a sensual quality; the semi-opaque tin glaze is perfectly suited to the form and just discovers the gentle warmth of the earthenware body beneath. It is a useful reminder that simplicity need not be dull[5].

In France, tin-glazed earthenware found further expression in Dufy's partnership with the Spanish ceramicist Artigas who set up his Paris studio in 1923. This mutually enriching partnership was to last for a decade. Dufy already had a strong interest in the applied arts having turned his hand to wood engraving, book illustration (for Apollinaire) and textile designs for Poiret. As well as vases decorated with flowers, fruit, fish and naiads, a series of very interesting miniature indoor gardens (*jardins de salon*) was commissioned by Nicholas Rubio Tuduri, an architect. These were slab-built, inspired by Japanese bonsai gardens and were each on a different theme: *le jardin toscan, le jardin de la marine, la course de taureaux, le jardin des naïades* and *le paradis terrestre*. As a technique, maiolica painting was eminently suited to Dufy's spontaneous, nervous style of painting: 'the painter in his fervour, has appropriated the bare surfaces of the walls in order to cover them with the fantasies of his imagination. The speed of loaded brush necessitated by this difficult medium, ineradicable, forces him to generous, confident execution of the design.'[6]

The 1925 Paris Exposition Internationale des Arts Décoratifs et Industriels marked the baptism of a new decorative aesthetic – Art Deco. French art pottery broadened its scope and several potters began to draw on the popular tradition of faience in their search for techniques which would translate well to the modern mood of the Deco style. Maurice Savin made tiles, plates and vases 'in the light-hearted spirit of Moustiers'[7] and also made tin-glazed and

Josep Llorens Artigas, Nicolas Rubio Tuduri and Raoul Dufy,
'Le jardin de la marine', 1923–6.
Collection Hopkins, Paris.
Courtesy of Anne Lajoix.

painted figure sculptures, in the line of the Della Robbias. Jean Mayodon's monumental ceramics – swimming pools, fountains, decorative panels and sculptures – portrayed neo-classical figures and achieved an antique bronze look with his liberal use of gold lustre on painted tin glaze. *Les Quatre Potiers*, members of the Favre family, sought the anonymity of early Renaissance potters. They worked in the pictorial tradition of tin glaze, making decorative and domestic wares, architectural panels (some with Léger), tiles and later, bathrooms and fireplaces. Industry too moved with the times; the faiencerie Henriot at Quimper employed, among others, Breton artist Mathurin Méheut to devise contemporary designs for tableware which was shown alongside the studio pottery at the 1925 exhibition.

By the 1950s, ceramics had welcomed yet more devotees from the art world – Léger at Biot; Chagall, Cocteau and Lurçat at Perpignan. Lurçat, a leading designer in the French tapestry revival of the 1930s and 1940s, produced some fine tin-glazed wares painted with animated animal and human symbolism. And then of course there was Picasso at Vallauris whose boundless creative energy sent waves throughout the pottery world and whose uninhibited approach to form and imagery set an example to a great number of contemporary potters concerned with decoration. Writing in 1953 in *House and Garden*, John Berger analysed the appeal of ceramics for artists: 'Painters are not concerned with trying to be potters or with studying the whole tradition of ceramics; rather they simply apply their plastic sensibility to the problems posed by the convex or concave surfaces presented to them.'

The overriding mood of these artists' ceramics is one of fun; simple, poetic imagery is communicated without any profound aesthetic pretensions. The mood was catching; the 1950 exhibition of Picasso's ceramics in London was the catalyst for a whole new contemporary style in studio ceramics in England. Alongside the Picasso influence, there was a postwar awareness of other cultures – Danish design began to appear in the shops; Mediterranean gastronomy

was brought to prominence through the publication of Elizabeth David's cookery books;[8] Italian-style espresso bars began to spring up everywhere. In ceramics, tin glaze, with its Mediterranean associations, was chosen as the primary medium for the expression of this new-found *joie-de-vivre*.

At the Central School of Art, Dora Billington, a Victorian in essence with a background of Stoke-on-Trent training, firmly believed in keeping all the pottery techniques alive, and in her teaching, gave equal emphasis to maiolica, slipware, stoneware and porcelain. William Newland, a part-time student of Billington's and teacher at the Institute of Education, nurtured a succession of budding potters – amongst them Margaret Hine and Nicholas Vergette – with

Jean Lurçat, pitcher, painted in blue, Perpignan circa 1951–66, Fitzwilliam Museum, Cambridge. © ADAGP, Paris and DACS, London 1993

whom he set up a studio. As a group they were dubbed the 'Picassettes'. The profile of Newland in Section III discusses both his and their work in more detail. Throwing was the main making method – animal and human figures were assembled from thrown parts, bowls were cut and altered. There was also a great revival of architectural ceramics. James Tower was another student of Newland at the Institute. He went on to exhibit exclusively with Gimpel Fils Gallery.

Maurice Savin, Cantatrice, ht. 44 cm, 1937.
Musée d'art moderne de la Ville de Paris © SPADEM 1993

James Tower, vase, ht 38 cm, white tin glaze over black glaze, 1957.
Tower used this 'double-glazing' technique (see p. 105), learned from Newland, throughout his career. The flattened vase form and black and white palette were also characteristic of Tower's work.
Courtesy of the Board of Trustees of the Victoria and Albert Museum.

Nicholas Vergette, bowl, ht 16.8 cm, 1954.
Coloured painting on tin glaze with sgraffito lines through the glaze.
Courtesy of the Board of Trustees of the Victoria and Albert Museum

Margaret Hine, Horse and Rider, ht 25 cm, 1949.
Thrown and assembled. Etched black glaze over tin glaze.
Collection William Newland

Kenneth Clark, dish, 1948.
Painted in manganese and pale blue.

From Newland, Tower learnt his particular method of double-glazing, whereby the fired tin glaze is coated with a black glaze which can then be scraped or etched back to the white (see p. 105 for description of technique). Stephen Sykes was another participant in the tin-glaze revival, making modelled figures and later substantial architectural panels.

Kenneth Clark was technician to Billington at the Central from 1949–50 and he also adopted the medium of tin-glazed earthenware. Like many others who started potting at that time, he was from a fine art background which predisposed him to an interest in colour. In the face of

considerable prejudice – colour was considered 'cheap' and 'industrial' by the Leach school – and inspired by Italian maiolica, he began to develop a bright palette for application to tin-glazed earthenware. The colours were crude but fitted in with the aesthetic of the day. In 1954 he married and began working with Ann Wyne Reeves, who had been a student at the Central School. Their London studio had previously belonged to Phyllis Keyes who had worked with Bell and Grant on many of their ceramic ventures. Under the occupation of the Clarks, the same studio played host to several visits from Professor Koyama, a distinguished Japanese scholar and champion of some of the first of the Japanese modern potters, who came to learn about techniques of maiolica. From the mid-1950s to the late 1970s, the Kenneth Clark Pottery was producing pressmoulded, slabbed and thrown individual pieces as well as tiles and murals. Today, in their Lewes studio, the main focus is on tile production. Apart from the likes of the Clarks, Newland and Caiger-Smith there was little tin-glaze work produced from the late 1960s until the mid-1980s, during which time the main centre of ceramic interest swung towards firstly domestic stoneware and then the serious, exploratory vessels of Britton, Poncelet, Fritsch and contemporaries.

Notes

1 Ruskin had been the first thinker.

2 Powolny himself had made a speciality of coy *putti* figures.

3 Much of the information on Metthey has been based on material in Françoise Espagnet's article, 'André Metthey et les Fauves', *Revue de la Céramique et du Verre*, No. 19, 1984.

4 Poiret used children of Ecole Martine to provide, through their art work, decorative material for his interior decoration studio, *cf*. essay by Fiona Macarthy in *The Omega Workshops*, Crafts Council catalogue, 1984.

5 Quoted in Judith Collins, 'Roger Fry and Omega Pottery', *Ceramic Review*, no. 86, 1984

6 From notes on Rubio's plans – translated from Lajoix, A., *La Céramique en France 1925–47*, Paris (Sous le Vent, 1983)

7 *cf*. Lajoix, op. cit.

8 Point made by Oliver Watson in his introduction to *British Studio Pottery*, *The Victoria and Albert Museum Collection*, Oxford (Phaidon-Christie's, 1990)

Other valuable sources for this chapter have been:

Houston, J., *Craft Classics Since the 1940s*, London (Crafts Council, 1988)

Houston, J., ed. and Cripps, David, *Lucie Rie*, London (Crafts Council, 1981)

Schweiger, W., *Wiener Werkstätte: Design in Vienna 1903–1932*, London (Thames and Hudson, 1984)

Kaller, J., *Viennese design and the Wiener Werkstätte*, New York (G. Brazillier in association with Galerie St Etienne, 1986)

Pinkham, R., *Catalogue of Pottery by William De Morgan*, London (Victoria and Albert Museum, 1973)

Ann Clark, owl dish, l. 41 cm, late 1950s..
Decorated with wax resist and oxides.

Opposite
Pippin Drysdale, detail of plate, maiolica painting with lustres, 'Carnevale Fruit series', 1992, Private collection.

SECTION II
Materials and Techniques

Whenever available, Seger (Unity) formulae have been given for glaze recipes. It has not always been possible to obtain precise analyses of American glaze materials, and in these cases I have either given approximate Seger formulae or suggested equivalent materials in the UK. The appendix on p. 168 gives formulae of the chief American and British frits, so that equivalents can be found.
All cone numbers refer to Orton cones. These can be read off against the chart on p. 169.

The Legacy of Piccolpasso

Through the ages several accounts have been written giving us information about materials and methods used in the making of tin-glazed earthenware.[1] In Europe, the earliest and most comprehensive of these is Cipriano Piccolpasso's *The Three Books of the Potter's Art*.[2] Not a potter by profession but an enthusiastic admirer of the maiolica for which his town was so famous in the High Renaissance, he wrote this complete handbook of Italian ceramic technology at Castel Durante in 1557 at the request of the Cardinal de Tournon. At that time, Italian maiolica techniques and styles were spreading throughout Europe and there must have been considerable need for technical guidelines.[3]

Thus clays, equipment, making methods, calcining and preparation of glaze materials, pigments and lustres, glazing and decorating, brushmaking, kilns and firing methods are all affectionately described and illustrated in remarkable detail. The treatise is not only a technical handbook for it also presents aesthetic guidelines within the accepted conventions of the day; standard wares are listed and patterns for decoration are illustrated, along with the prices paid for their execution. Much of the information, particularly that concerned with glaze composition concerns local materials and will only give us general indications – which potter today will calcine his own alkaline frit from sand and ashes of wine-lees? The recipes given by Piccolpasso were intended as working instructions and fall far short of the accurate analyses we would expect today. However, the overall tenets of tin-glazed earthenware practice were similar throughout its history and are still applicable today. In the first part of this chapter, I propose to discuss the essential materials – clays, glazes and pigments, as well as kilns, both from a historical and contemporary point of view. The second part is of a more practical nature and deals with techniques of glazing, decorating and firing.

Materials and Kilns

Clays

The traditional body for tin glaze was a natural clay containing iron oxide and a high proportion of chalk (calcium carbonate) – usually somewhere between 15 and 22%[4]. This type of clay is referred to as a true marl[5] or more specifically, malm.[6] The East Anglian and Kentish gault clays used by London delftware potters are examples of English malms. Piccolpasso talks of *genga* (chalky clay) which is 'white and light'. There were several advantages to using this type of body for tin glaze. The lime component acts as a bleach on the red iron in the clay and the body fires to a pale buff colour. The need for a very densely opacified glaze (and expensive tin) was therefore reduced. Calcium also has a high coefficient of expansion (third highest after soda and potash) which gives high contraction on cooling, thus putting the glaze under compression and preventing crazing. The fired body is remarkably pale in comparison to red bodies. This type of body also has a low maturing temperature and little tolerance for marginal overfiring. Above 1100°C, the calcium becomes a very active flux and will rapidly cause the body to fuse and distort. This was obviously not a problem for the wood-fired wares of 16th century Italy which would not have been fired much higher than 1000°C. The high-lime body was not used for cooking pots as it became very brittle with constant thermal expansion and contraction and a red clay was found to be more suitable for this purpose. If a malm clay contained so much lime that it had a refractory nature and would not harden on its own, then it was mixed with a common red clay to render it more fusible. Spanish potteries traditionally use a mixture of calcareous and red clays or just add lime to local red clay. Potters, such as the Dutch delftware makers, who did not have direct access to high-lime marls, made their own mixtures of imported malms and local clays. André Metthey also describes his own blend of local clays (see p.68), not dissimilar to the composition of Paris faience described by Bastenaire-Daudenart and quoted by Caiger-Smith.[7] Some of the more peasant-type maiolica – Moroccan for example – is entirely red-bodied. There is no off-the-peg equivalent to the gault clays available today in England. The following recipes are examples of high-lime bodies maturing at low temperature:

William Gordon Maiolica Bodies (1961)

Ball clay	80	Ball clay	50
Quartz	20	Lime	30
Lime	50	China clay	20

Maturing 900°C to 940°C

With today's sophisticated ceramic technology and demand for stronger higher-fired bodies and harder glazes, a wide variety of bodies can be used and the crazing problems associated with soft-fired bodies do not tend to arise. A good low-firing body is Fremington clay, high in soda and potash and normally beginning to bloat at about 1080°C. It is used by Caiger-Smith who adds dolomite for firing stability (see p. 108). Most commercial red earthenwares are strong, resistant to thermal shock and have a wide firing range, with maturity limits ranging from 1040–1160°C. Provided the glaze is well adjusted, glaze fit is not usually a problem. Red clays tend to fire very dark above 1100°C. Mixtures of buff and red clays can produce warm apricot tones but usually require a firing of 1120°C or more to avoid crazing in the glaze. White earthenware bodies give an excellent base for tin glaze (and you can get away with a thinner glaze application) but most require a bisque temperature of at least 1160°C for a good subsequent glaze fit. Most North American tin-glaze potters prefer to blend their own bodies and examples of these are given in Section III.

One important factor in the choice of a body, apart from glaze fit, is the effect of the body on the colour of the glaze, particularly in the high-earthenware range. On a red body the glaze will appear cooler and greyer; warmer and creamier on a buff or white body. Scumming can be a problem on red bodies, particularly those high in calcium. This refers to whitish-yellow deposits caused by the crystallisation of soluble salts when the water evaporates and readily visible at the dry or biscuit stage. These areas are often less porous and can affect absorption of the glaze. The addition of 1–2% barium carbonate (poisonous substance) to a body at the blunging stage will render the salts insoluble thus eliminating the problem.[8] Five to ten per cent talc can also be added to lower the maturing temperature and increase resistance to thermal shock.

Glazes

The early Middle Eastern tin glazes were alkaline-based, soft, highly fusible and liable to craze, although when the frit-paste body was developed with its high shrinkage the glaze fit was radically improved. European tin glazes were lead-based with alkaline additions and this combination produced more durable, stable glazes. The Italian and Dutch methods of tin glazing differed considerably from those of other countries in that a mattish very opaque tin white glaze (Piccolpasso calls it the *color* or *bianco*) was used underneath a transparent shiny overglaze (*coperta* in Italian, *kwaart* in Dutch). This procedure might well have evolved from slipware techniques. In maiolica it served several purposes: on a relatively dry glaze surface the fine lines and shaded washes of the painting would not run and distort; refractory pigments such as antimony-based yellows and oranges and natural earths (e.g. ochres) normally rough to the touch on a fired glaze, would be glossed over by the shiny overglaze; and firing temperatures were not as crucial as they would have been with a single fusible glaze. The thin *coperta* was more tolerant of variation in temperature and would affect the movement of pigments less. With Dutch delftware, the hard shine of the *kwaart* brought the appearance of the wares ever closer to that of Chinese porcelain.

All the glazes described by Piccolpasso, with their regional variations, are essentially combinations of lead and alkaline fluxes and silica. There was little or no alumina content and the Italians seem to have been unaware of the valuable properties of clay (containing both alumina and silica) in glaze composition. However, this lack of alumina would not have posed undue problems at such low-firing temperatures. An alkaline frit known as the *marzacotto* served as a main constituent of both the *bianco* and the *coperta*, and as a flux for pigments. The alkaline component came from wine lees, the sediment left in the cask after the wine has been drawn off. The lees were collected, dried and burned to create the ashes which contain up to 90% potassium carbonate.[9] These were then mixed with sand in an approximate ratio of one to three, fired in the kiln and then finely milled. The 'best' sand of San Giovanni in Tuscany is described by Piccolpasso 'as white, glittering like silver, heavy clear and clean' and is probably silica sand. Sands however can vary enormously in composition (e.g. marble and granite sands) and, depending on their source, may well have brought in other oxides such as those of calcium, magnesium and aluminium. To make the *bianco*, the *marzacotto* was combined with lead-tin ash. Lead-tin ash is itself a fritted mixture of lead metal and tin metal, calcined and then crushed and levigated to separate the light, white ash from the heavier unoxidised particles.[10] The combination of *marzacotto* and lead-tin ash was then milled, fritted and milled again to make the *bianco*. Such repeated calcining and milling helped to produce some of the highest quality glazes and pigments. The *coperta* required lead and salt to be added to the ingredients of the *marzacotto*, thereby bringing in extra fluxes. Venetian maiolica did not use the *coperta*, preferring instead a more fusible tin glaze, and most

78

other European countries seem to have rejected the complexities of double glazing. The *coperta* technique was tiresome in that it was an extra process and there was sometimes a problem of lifting-off from the base glaze. To avoid this, the *coperta* was usually applied by means of flicking or spraying.

Tin glazes were often tinted in imitation of porcelain, although the Della Robbia coloured glazes were an isolated early example of a different kind. Venice, Delft, Nevers, London and Bristol among others all used coloured tin glazes, ranging from the pale buff (manganese) base of *bianco sopra bianco* and the lavender blue (impure cobalt – *zaffre*) of the *berretino* to the dark blues of Nevers, London, Delft and Habaner wares. There have also been antimony-stained oranges and manganese and iron dark browns and blacks. Paradoxically, tiny amounts of manganese were sometimes added to make the glaze seem whiter.

There are several differences in contemporary glaze practice. One is in the wide firing range adopted by earthenware potters today. For a variety of reasons, there is a tremendous range of glaze-firing temperatures from 950°C right up to 1140°C. Today's frits are safer and more reliable than their 16th century equivalents. Many glazes are lead-free, and the opacifier zirconium silicate is widely used as a viable and cheaper alternative to tin oxide.

Glaze Composition Today

Tin-glaze composition today is broadly similar to Piccolpasso's except that it is based on commercially prepared frits – lead bisilicate, lead sesquisilicate and borax and alkaline frits. The frits are often used in combinations so as to create a stable complex silicate. As in Piccolpasso's day, fritting entails calcination of the flux i.e. lead, borax, soda or potash, with silica and often other ingredients, to produce an insoluble, homogenous, glass-like material. Tables I and II on p.168 give examples of the range of commercial frits available and their composition.

Colour response, texture and opacity are all factors determined by the nature of the primary fluxes (lead, soda, potash, boric oxide), by the addition of the so-called secondary fluxes (whiting, zinc, barium, magnesium, bone ash) and by the ratio of alumina to silica (in the Seger Molecular Formula, a 1:10 ratio, for example, is an average ratio for a clear shiny glaze).

Fluxes

The dominant flux in the glaze will be one of the main factors in determining the surface quality and type of colour response.

Lead frits (bisilicate and sesquisilicate) The advantages of using lead frits in the glaze are:
1 elasticity and low coefficient of expansion, thus minimising crazing;
2 bright smooth surface with deep soft shine;
3 stabilising, slow maturing qualities with good smoothing-over after release of gases;
4 good colour response in certain areas, notably antimony yellows and oranges, and copper greens.

The disadvantages are:
1 Toxicity: underfired lead glazes or those with too high a lead content can produce lead release, particularly in association with copper, and are therefore dangerous. All lead-based glazes for domestic ware should be tested for lead release (see p. 100). American regulations on lead release factors are more stringent than in the UK and, as can be seen from their glaze recipes, most North American tin-glaze potters use entirely lead-free glazes.
2 High lead content can dissolve the tin oxide and reduce opacity.
3 Sometimes unexciting colour response due to the modifying yellowness of lead.

An example of a lead frit tin glaze is:

Lead bisilicate	80
China clay	10
Tin oxide	10
(1020–1060°C)	

Seger molecular formula:

PbO 1.00	Al$_2$O$_3$ 0.25	SiO$_2$ 2.19
		SnO$_2$ 0.28

Alkaline frits have a high coefficient of expansion and are therefore prone to crazing. They

79

tend to be unstable and lacking in fired strength. They also produce a more fuzzy reaction to colouring oxides. On the positive side, their milkiness creates a good starting point for opacification and they promote a brilliant colour response with certain oxides – copper, for example, will give turquoise hues, manganese a rich plummy purple.

Borax frits are very useful either on their own or in conjunction with lead frits. Boric oxide has a low coefficient of expansion and will therefore discourage crazing. It also helps to produce a balanced glaze. It will whiten a lead glaze and give brighter colour response. Lead borosilicates are much used in industrial glazes for their all-round qualities.

An example of a glaze based on alkaline and borax frits is:

High alkaline frit (P 2250)	23
Standard borax frit (P 2953)	55
China clay	15
Tin oxide	8
Zirconium silicate	6
(1080–1100°C)	

Seger molecular formula:

KNaO	0.53	Al_2O_3	0.32	SiO_2	2.18
CaO	0.47	B_2O_3	0.42	ZrO_2	0.10
				SnO_2	0.16

Calcium borate frit Colemanite appears in many American recipes. It is a natural frit, borocalcite, and introduces boric oxide and calcium to a glaze. In the UK, it is advisable to substitute calcium borate frit as the form of colemanite available here is quite soluble and will cause 'spluttering' of the glaze (usually on to the kiln shelf!). Calcium borate frit is useful in small quantities as a balancing flux, to encourage opacity and resist crazing. Large amounts will dull the colours. Gerstley borate is another American material similar to colemanite but which also contains soda. Calcium borate frit would be a close approximation.

White opaque zircon-borax frits are useful as a starting point for a maiolica-type glaze. They generally have a high calcium and zinc content.

Lithium, in the naturally fritted forms of lithium carbonate or lithium felspar, has valuable quali-ties in low-temperature glazes. It has twice the fluxing power, weight for weight, of soda and potash and it also has a lower rate of expansion and it will therefore inhibit crazing.

Felspars and Secondary Fluxes

Felspars are often used in tin glazes because of their complex composition, thus introducing alkaline fluxes, chiefly soda and potash, as well as alumina and silica into the glaze. Cornish stone in particular encourages opacification. Zinc (2–3%) increases hardness, shine and opacity and in larger amounts (8–10%) produces a pleasing silky matt crystalline surface. In association with soda, potash and calcia, it intensifies blues and copper greens but it tends to have a muddy effect on other colouring oxides, in particular chrome. Up to 10% whiting (calcium carbonate) in a glaze will improve durability and reduce lead solubility. Larger amounts will promote opacity and produce a crystalline matt surface. Talc (magnesium silicate) and barium carbonate have good anti-craze properties and will encourage matt opaque crystalline surfaces.

Opacifiers

Opacification then is favoured by certain conditions in the glaze. It obviously requires more to opacify a transparent, glassy glaze than one which is already stiff and crystalline. A glaze which is not rendered fully opaque by the addition of 10% tin oxide could readily be altered in composition to create a more conducive base for opacification e.g. by increasing the China clay or Cornish stone content or by adding small percentages of barium or talc. The degree of opacity is also dependent on the degree of fusion in the glaze. Although tin glazes are very stable and have a wide firing range, they will be matter and a much denser white at the lower end of the range, translucent and lustrous at the top end. The main opacifying agents are:

Tin oxide (SnO_2 – stannic oxide, tin dioxide) Tin oxide creates opacity through its undissolved particles remaining in suspension in the glaze. Traditional tin glazes often contained as much as 20% tin oxide. Such large amounts of tin increase the viscosity of the glaze and can cause pinholing, crawling and mattness. Eight to ten per cent is a more typical addition today if the glaze is well adjusted (see above). For many potters, tin gives an unrivalled quality of opacity with a soft, milky whiteness. The main drawback is its facility for attracting chrome. Any form of chromium oxide in the kiln will migrate and form pink flashes on the glaze surface. Similarly, pigments containing chrome (and many commercial stains do) used on the tin glaze will tend to create an unpleasant yellow halo. Chrome-tin pink stains and glazes make positive use of this property. Heavy reduction of a tin-opacified glaze will make the glaze turn grey.

Zirconium silicate ($ZrSiO_4$) Zirconium silicate is now commonly used as an opacifier, either on its own or in combination with tin. It produces a more crystalline opacity than tin and has high craze-resistance. It is considerably cheaper than tin (at the time of writing, Ceramatech quoted 1kg tin oxide at almost four times the cost of 1kg of Zircosil 5). Very fine grades of zirconium silicate which give excellent opacity with 10–15% are now on the market. Zircosil 5 (replacing the old Disperzon) is commonly used in the UK, Zircopax or Superpax in the USA. In comparison with tin, the quality of whiteness imparted by zirconium silicate tends to be harsher and the sensitivity of colour response is not so acute. Tiny additions of rutile ($\frac{1}{2}$–2%) can be added to soften the hard whiteness. It is redeemed by its tolerance of chrome and its good behaviour in reduction. It is therefore most suitable as a base for those using primarily commercial stains. Alan Peascod (see p. 118) is a champion of zircon claiming it produces superior whites, thus demonstrating that ultimately the choice is a matter of personal preference and fitness for purpose.

Titanium dioxide (TiO_2) Creates opacity by crystal formation within the glaze. Used in small amounts (3–5%), in combination with other opacifiers, it will give a creamy tone and rich satin surface to the glaze. Colour response is consequently modified but in a subtle rather than a dull way (particularly noticeable with cobalt). Titanium picks up on iron in the body and on a red body will create warm iron browns where the glaze is thin. The presence of titanium is favourable for all iron pigments. As seen above, rutile, which is a natural form of iron-bearing titanium, is sometimes used in tiny amounts to soften the whiteness of a glaze.

Pigments

Piccolpasso describes five basic pigments used for maiolica: three compound and two natural colours. There were also variations and intermixtures of these basic pigments, creating an incredibly varied palette. They could be applied 'light or dark as pleases the painter' – one only has to look at the painting on the *istoriato* pieces to have evidence of the degree of shading and blending that was customary. As with the glazes, the high quality and fine texture of these colours was achieved by repeated mixing, calcining and milling, something we could do much more of today.

Piccolpasso's pigments:

Green
The green was a base (*ramina*) consisting of a calcined mixture of copper, sulphur and salt. The *ramina* was then further compounded with antimony and lead and fired again. The fluxes would help to dilute the strength of copper and make for greater stability of application. The refractory antimony would also help to fix the volatile copper.

Orange
Iron rust (best from ships' anchors, we are told) was calcined, sometimes with sulphur, and quenched in urine to 'purify' it. It was then compounded with lead and antimony and lees, calcined again and milled.

Yellow
This was a compound of antimony, lead, lees and common salt, fritted and ground.

The two natural pigments were:

Zaffre (CoO)
An impure form of cobalt oxide containing traces of other elements and slightly fusible. Piccolpasso tells us it came from Venice and that the 'good sort is that which is of a violet tawny cast'.

Manganese (pyrolusite, MnO_2)

Also quite fusible on its own. These two natural pigments did not require calcining, just grinding.

Piccolpasso goes on to describe in detail pigments used in *istoriato* painting. He tells us, for example, that a mixture of light yellow and white pigment (tin) was used 'to simulate a dawn, dead flesh, rocks and certain roads that are in a bright light' and that a mixture of copper (*ramina*) and light yellow was good for 'verdant meadows and certain bushes'

The range of colours available to us today has been considerably widened by the discoveries of chrome, vanadium and nickel oxides, and by a wide range of proprietary stains. Endless combinations are possible – both within the oxides and between the oxides and the commercial colours. The oxides tend to give us good blues, greens, ochres and browns; brighter colours, such as reds and yellows, can most easily be obtained from the commercial range. The two can complement each other quite well; the oxides subtle and variable in intensity; the commercial stains stable and predictable but on their own sometimes crude and bland.

Colouring oxides for maiolica painting today

Cobalt oxide (CoO) or carbonate (CoCO$_3$) A powerful oxide and flux. The slightly less strong carbonate has the advantage of a distinctive pink colour in the raw state (and is therefore easily identifiable). The fired colour of the cobalt oxide available today is much brighter and cruder than in Piccolpasso's day. It is however easily toned down with one of the modifying oxides such as nickel or manganese, or a little red clay. Cobalt is the most susceptible of the colouring oxides to breaking up and texturing on a thick tin glaze. It is one of the most concentrated colours and therefore is best diluted with some flux and/or China clay to prevent a rough metallic surface where thick. It is a good liner colour.

Copper oxide (CuO) or carbonate (CuCO$_3$)
The carbonate is not easily assimilated by water although this can be helped by a drop of washing-up liquid. It is a strong oxide, less stable than cobalt and also a flux. It dissolves readily and tends to fuzz into the surrounding glaze and is therefore not suitable for fine lines or precision painting, but it is good as a filler. It can be modified with a number of oxides – e.g. iron, nickel, rutile, manganese, to interesting effect. It turns bright turquoise when used on an alkaline glaze.

Manganese dioxide (MnO$_2$) or carbonate (MnCO$_3$) It produces purplish-browns to black on lead-based glazes, pink to plum purple on alkaline-dominated glazes. It is weaker than cobalt and copper and it has a pronounced speckle. It only acts as a flux above 1080°C. It is good as a mixer and modifier.

Red iron oxide (ferric oxide, Fe$_2$O$_3$) It produces a grainy reddish brown on tin glaze. The presence of zinc or zirconium in the glaze will dull the colour response, producing more murky browns. Titanium is favourable to iron, yielding rich oranges and yellows. Interesting bronzy tones can be obtained when mixed with copper. Iron and nickel will give a rich browny-black.

Nickel oxide (NiO) It produces a khaki green on tin glaze. It is a excellent modifier of cobalt and copper. It is strong and very refractory so it needs adequate dilution with flux.

Rutile (TiO$_2$) This is an impure form of titanium dioxide with traces of iron. If used on its own, it needs to be well fluxed as it is very refractory. It gives a slightly grainy yellow ochre colour on tin glaze. It is an interesting modifier of cobalt (to give air force blues) and copper (to give lustrous leafy green). It produces good oranges with iron and a pink tinge when used on an alkaline glaze.

Ilmenite (ferrous titanate, FeTiO$_3$) This is coarser than rutile with a variable higher iron content. It can be used in similar ways to rutile but it will produce a more pronounced speckle.

Chromium oxide (Cr$_2$O$_3$) On its own it produces a rather flat 'park bench' green. On a tin-opacified glaze, there is often an unpleasant yellow staining the surrounding glaze. The presence of zinc will turn the chrome brown. Chrome is most useful in its capacity for producing chrome-tin pinks and reds (see p. 85). Chrome is extensively used in the preparation of stains and underglaze colours. Potassium dichromate ($K_2Cr_2O_7$) is a soluble and therefore highly poisonous form.

Antimony oxide (Sb_2O_3) In combination with lead, it produces the traditional maiolica egg yellow colour (see below).

Vanadium oxide (vanadium pentoxide, V_2O_5)
This is much used in the preparation of proprietary stains. It will give yellows on a lead-based glaze, but it is little used in straight maiolica painting as it is both highly refractory and a weak colourant.

It is important to learn to exploit the potential of each pigment; cobalt is strong and stable and therefore suitable as a liner colour; copper is very volatile and fuzzy – unsuitable for fine lines but effective on larger areas; iron mixtures have a granular appearance, etc. Different surface textures will also be created according to how refractory or fluxing the pigments are – rutile mixtures, for example, have to be used with care as they can become rough and blistered if too thick, but appropriately applied can create a satin film which is pleasing to the touch.

Different qualities can be produced by the use of metal sulphates – copper, cobalt and manganese sulphates. As these are in solution, they suffuse the glaze to give a very soft effect. The crystals need to be dissolved in a minimal amount of hot water prior to use.

The pigments I use are mostly mixed by volume and have additions of flux and/or China clay, depending on the nature of the oxide and the effect I want to achieve. Refractory pigments such as rutile, nickel, chrome and antimony will obviously require more flux. A good all-purpose flux to use is a standard borax frit which will generally benefit colours. Alkaline frit will help to encourage copper blues and manganese purples. Lead bisilicate is good with rutile and ilmenite mixtures. It is also possible to use the base tin glaze as a pigment flux, but its whiteness will make the colours more pastel. Most commercial stains and underglaze colours are refractory and a good mixing guide here would be one part stain/one part frit (by volume). The colours are mixed with water, sieved through 80s then 200s mesh, and kept in airtight jars. Caiger-Smith grinds his pigments on tiles with a palette knife. They are mixed with a little gum-arabic solution for improved flow, and left to harden. They can then be used in the way that a watercolour palette would be. There is more information about painting mediums on p.93. + p. 94

Many pigments benefit from calcining and/or grinding. The purpose of calcining is to bring out the best colour and remove potentially harmful gaseous compounds.[11] Some of the commercially available oxides such as those of copper and cobalt have not been sufficiently oxidised, and will give a greatly improved colour if calcined and ground in a ball mill with water for 2–4 hours. Optimum calcining temperatures vary[12] but a low biscuit temperature (I have calcined successfully at 970°C) would be a good starting point and means that, as in Piccolpasso's day, pigments can be calcined in the biscuit firing. Cobalt and manganese are quite coarse and undissolved particles produce prominent specking if used as bought. This can be eliminated by 1–2 hours of ball milling. (For those who do not have access to a ball mill, a pestle and mortar can be used, but it is much harder work!).

Maiolica painters come to develop their own palette of colours. It is a sad fact that with the same kind of commercial stains available universally, their range of often rather obvious colours seems to be an increasingly common denominator. Regionalism and individuality in terms of colours is rare. Initially prepared for industrial use, there is much in the indiscriminate use of these colours that intimates a standardisation and refinement which dissociates them from (in Rawson's words) the 'earthy nature of ceramic materials'. There is much to be said for the practice of making up one's own pigments to accord with a personal vision. This can be approached at the simple level of empirically mixing oxides and stains as already mentioned; or it can be approached in a more scientific way, by careful balancing of ingredients, calcining and milling. Calcination brings into play the effects of modifying agents (e.g. zinc, tin, zirconium and titanium), fluxes and silica, which, compounded with the colouring oxide, produce colours of a stability and diversity unobtainable through the simple oxides. These are in fact the basic constituents of commercial stains, but can be freely compounded to create an individually-based palette. For anyone interested in pursuing this option, I recommend Kenneth Shaw's *Ceramic Colours and Pottery Decoration* which contains a useful chapter on colour making for the studio potter.

Below is a chart of some basic oxide mixtures which I made and tested for use in my work. There are hundreds of other possible combinations. The proportions are all by volume and the mixtures are sieved twice through an 80s mesh sieve (200s mesh for cobalt mixtures).

OXIDE MIXTURES TABLE

MIXTURES (from left to right in the illustration on p. 86)	Cobalt oxide	Copper oxide	Manganese dioxide	Red iron oxide	Nickel oxide	Rutile	Ilmenite	Chromium oxide	Yellow ochre	Lemon yellow stain	Borax frit	Alkaline frit	Lead bisilicate	China clay	Red clay	COLOUR NB: All mixtures are by volume (e.g. teaspoons)
1						1							2			Ochre yellow
2				1		3							3			orange rust
3						1			1							lustrous yellow
4				2	1						2					brown-black
5			1			1½					2					donkey brown
6	1			1				½			2					blue-black
7		½	1											1		grey-green
8		1												1		green/turquoise
9		½										1	1			yellowy-green
10	1	1	½	½							2					dark blue green
11		1				2					2					sage green
12		1								1	1					strong green
13		¼	2								1					bronze green
14				1							1					khaki
15	1										1			1		strong blue
16	1										1				1	darker blue
17	1					1					1					textured blue-green-grey
18	1						1				1					speckled strong blue*
19	1				¼						1					grey-blue
20	½	1											2	½		purple-blue
21	1	1									1			1		greeny-blue

*Speckle more pronounced if ilmenite is not sieved.

Pigments (see photograph on p. 86) were tested on two different glazes, fired to 1080°C (Cone 03):

Glaze A: (satin-cream titanium, adaptation of Caiger-Smith 057 glaze)

Lead bisilicate	61	Zinc oxide	2
Zircon-borax frit	9	Tin oxide	4
Cornish stone	13	Zirconium silicate	3
China clay	5	Titanium dioxide	3

Seger molecular formula:

PbO	0.73	Al_2O_3	0.24	SiO_2	2.56
$KNaO$	0.09	B_2O_3	0.08	TiO_2	0.15
CaO	0.07			ZrO_2	0.10
ZnO	0.11			SnO_2	0.11

Glaze B: (from Victor Bryant – leadless, zirconium-opacified)

Zircon-borax frit	78	Nepheline syenite	14
China clay	5	Bentonite	2
Whiting	5	Zirconium silicate	5

Seger molecular formula:

$KNaO$	0.38	Al_2O_3	0.33	SiO_2	3.28
CaO	0.54	B_2O_3	0.59	ZrO_2	0.31
ZnO	0.08				

Antimony yellows and oranges

Whilst it is relatively easy today to obtain similar blues and greens to those of Italian maiolica, the rich egg yellows and burnt oranges obtained from antimony are without parallel in modern commercial stains and need to be prepared in the studio. Below are some modern recipes for these pigments. Antimony yellow is sometimes referred to as Naples yellow. These pigments should not be fired higher than 1060°C as above this temperature the colour will fade.

Naples Yellow (from Reptile)

by weight

Antimony oxide	5½
Lead oxide	10
Tin oxide	3

DC Yellow

by weight

Litharge (or red lead)	2½
Antimony oxide	1
plus some tin-glaze slop	

DC Orange

As above plus 1½ ferrous sulphate crystals – melt in hot water before adding to other ingredients

Naples yellow (from *Industrial Ceramics* by Singer and Singer)

Red lead	60%
Tin oxide	20%
Antimony oxide	20%

Calcine at 950°C and then grind finely (preferably overnight) and sieve through 200s mesh.

For orange, add 5% red iron oxide.

Chrome-tin Pinks And Reds

Chrome-tin pinks and reds are favoured by a base glaze with predominant fluxes of lead and lime. Alumina content should be low as this material deadens the red colour. Zinc in the glaze will turn the stain brown. The colour of the stain is influenced by its constituents: silica will encourage a bluish red; lime a deep red; boric oxide a lilac shade. Chrome-tin stains tend to volatilise above 1080°C.

Recipes (from *Ceramic Colours and Pottery Decoration* by Shaw)

Tin oxide	50
Whiting	25
Flint	18
Borax	4
Potassium dichromate	3

Very red

Tin oxide	86
Whiting	60
Flint	47
Fluorspar	19
Potassium dichromate	4

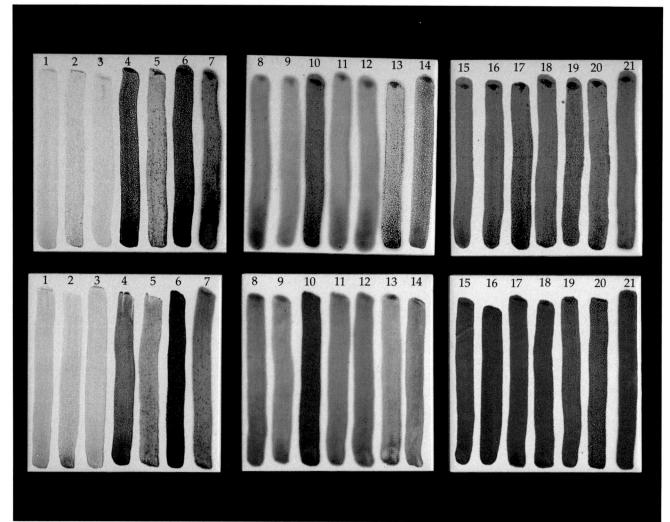

Glaze A

Glaze B

Colour tests showing basic oxide mixtures on two glazes: the titanium in glaze A (top row) has softened and modified the colours, particularly noticeable with the blues, and has favoured the iron pigments. Glaze B (bottom row) is whiter and, being leadless, has produced a more alkaline-type colour response, notably with the copper pigments.
(See table on p. 84.)

The stains should be blended and ground (in a pestle and mortar) with water, omitting the potassium dichromate. For the recipe containing borax (soluble), do not pour off any excess water. The potassium dichromate should be dissolved in boiling water and added to the mixture. Grind again and calcine to at least 1100°C (and, for stability, at least to a temperature greater than that of your glaze firing). Sieve through 200s mesh.

Reduced-Pigment Lustres

Piccolpasso gives a description of the painting and firing of lustreware (which he refers to as 'maiolica' – this appellation obviously still being closely linked with Hispano-Moresque forerunners) as carried out at Gubbio. Deruta was the other main centre of lustreware. He explains that certain areas were left blank at the time of in-glaze painting so that they could be filled in later with lustre. He gives recipes for red and gold lustre pigments (A and B below). The ingredients were ground, left to dissolve in vinegar and ground again before painting.

	A	B
Red earth	3oz	6oz
Armenian bole*	1oz	–
Ferreto of Spain**	2oz	3oz
Cinnabar***	–	3oz

To recipe B is also added one silver *carlino* (coin) to make the gold colour.

* a natural very bright red clay used in Isnik decoration
** most probably copper sulphide
***mercuric sulphide or vermilion (it might have assisted reduction, according to Caiger-Smith)

It is curious that the technique of lustres on tin glaze was neither used extensively in Italy nor was it transplanted to other countries which grew out of the Italian tradition. Caiger-Smith explains the phenomenon as one of stylistic incompatability:

> The Italians never used lustre with the vigour and naturalness of the Arabic and Spanish potters. Its flat reflecting surface was perhaps in better agreement with abstract or formalised designs than with the fine outline drawing with modulated tones of colour which became the special skill of the Italian painters.[13]

According to those who practise it, the technique of reduced-pigment lustres is hazardous and the results tantalisingly unpredictable. It is therefore not surprising that few potters actively engage with the process. Alan Caiger-Smith, Alan Peascod and Sutton Taylor all use lustre on tin glaze, and Sutton Taylor's current practice is unusual in that he uses stannous oxide (tin monoxide SnO) instead of the usual stannic oxide (tin dioxide SnO_2). Stannous oxide, while still providing the chemical reactions of tin, does not act as an opacifier and slips can thus be seen through the glaze. It is not within the scope of this book to go into the many variables and

Sutton Taylor, footed bowl, diam 51 cm, 1992.
Reduced-pigment lustres on high-fired earthenware with transparent stannous oxide glaze. The cloudy effects are made by overpainting areas with the same base glaze but with stannic oxide. The stannous oxide (tin monoxide – SnO) acts as a flux and is quicker to dissolve in the glaze than the more commonly used opacifying stannic oxide (tin dioxide – SnO_2), but it still favours the formation of lustres.

Cipriano Piccolpasso, drawing, the firing of the kiln, from
The Three Books of the Potter's Art, *1557.*
Courtesy of the Board of Trustees of the Victoria and Albert
Museum

Cipriano Piccolpasso, drawing, the arrangement of flatware on
spurs in the saggar, from The Three Books of The Potter's
Art, *1557. Courtesy of the Board of Trustees of the Victoria and*
Albert Museum.

complexities of reduced-pigment lustre and for anyone wishing to attempt it, I would recommend Alan Caiger-Smith's *Lustre Pottery* as a comprehensive handbook of both historical and contemporary techniques. The profile of Caiger-Smith (pp. 106–12) includes a short account of his lustre procedure and the profile of Alan Peascod also contains comments about his use of the technique.

Kilns

The traditional type of kiln was a wood-fired, updraught design (see drawing above), with a large firebox directly under the firing chamber. Arches supported the floor of the chamber. The flames passed straight up through the wares and out of the vent ports in the arched roof. There were four spy-holes in the side wall. Willow was the main source of wood (used today by Caiger-Smith). This design of kiln would only have

been suitable for the customary firings of 950–1000°C; neither the design nor the bricks would have withstood higher temperatures. It would also be difficult to retain heat long enough to produce a significant rise in temperature. The unevenness of heat inevitable in an updraught kiln was accommodated by the firing of different types of ware in appropriate places. Glazed wares had the pride of place where temperatures were most predictable. Corners and odd, very hot or very cold, places were filled with raw ware and containers of mixtures for calcining. Saggars protected the glazed ware from fly-ash and from the blistering effects of the direct flame. Dishes were fired upside down, their rims resting on three spurs, and the scars are visible on many of the old pots. Much of the cruder Mediterranean tin-glaze ware is still fired in similar fashion today.

The type of kiln described by Piccolpasso has remained the standard design of earthenware kiln in the Mediterranean countries. Although most factories and large-scale concerns now have more sophisticated equipment at their disposal, many of the rural potteries still have kilns very similar to Piccolpasso's. Most studio potters working in tin glaze have electric kilns, to which there are obvious advantages – they are reliable, easy to operate, and leave the potter free to get on with other tasks. Wood-firing will however give certain effects that are not possible in a totally oxidised firing. Caiger-Smith is the main exponent of wood-fired tin glaze and his procedures are discussed in the profile (pp. 106–12). His kiln is of a more sophisticated design than Piccolpasso's – the semi-circular vault and cross-draught almost eliminating altogether the usual problems associated with this type of firing (see drawing p. 109).

Tin-glazed earthenware has always been twice-fired. This is because tin glazes, being of a high viscosity, have a tendency to crawl if used in mono-firing. The traditional Continental procedure is to fire the bisque higher than the glost. With the high-lime body, this ensures that the clay is fired to its maturing point, giving a tighter, stronger, more craze-proof body. The lower glaze temperature ensures maximum colour response, stability of glaze and therefore less distortion of painting. Most Continental workshops and factories still follow this fairly foolproof method and average firing temperatures are in the region of 1000°C for bisque, 950°C for glost.

Notes

1 These include:
Kashan potter Abu'l-Qasim's Treatise on Ceramics (translated by J.W. Allan, *Iran*, vol. 11, 1973 pp.111–20)
Gerrit Paape, *De Plateelbakker of Delftsch Aardewerk Makker* (1794)
Pierre-Paul Caussy, *L'Art de la Fayence* (Rouen, circa 1730) manuscript in the Musée départementale breton, Quimper.
Bastenaire-Daudenart, F., *La Faïence* (Paris, 1828)
L'Art de Fabriquer la Faïence Blanche (1830)
There were numerous others in the 19th century.

2 Cipriano Piccolpasso, *The Three Books of the Potter's Art*, facsimile edition with translation and commentary by R.Lightbown and Alan Caiger-Smith, London (Scolar Press, 1980).

3 Ibid. – commentary

4 From Brongniart's analyses of clays as quoted in Caiger-Smith, A., *Tin-glaze Pottery in Europe and the Islamic World*, London (Faber and Faber, 1973.)

5 Many iron-bearing clays are today referred to as marls e.g. Etruria Marl, but they contain little or no lime.

6 See Hamer, Frank, *The Potter's Dictionary of Materials and Techniques*, Second Edition, London (A & C Black, 1986) for further information on marls.

7 Caiger-Smith, A., *Tin-glaze Pottery in Europe and the Islamic World*

8 Fraser, H., *Ceramic Faults and Their Remedies*, London (A & C Black, 1986)

9 Commentary to Piccolpasso, see (2)

10 Parmelee, C. W., *Ceramic Glazes*, Chicago, 1951. Hamer, op. cit., explains the process of levigation as 'the process of passing a thin slurry through a series of traps where the heavier particles settle and the finer particles overflow'.

11 Shaw, Kenneth, *Ceramic Colours and Pottery Decoration*, London (Faber and Faber, 1968)

12 Ibid. Gives optimum calcining temperatures for different oxides.

13 Commentary to Piccolpasso

Other sources of reference:

Singer, F. and Singer, S.S., *Industrial Ceramics* (Chapman and Hall, 1963) – good section on pigment composition.
'The Lure of Lustre', Clive Fiddis, *Ceramic Review*, nos 61 and 62, 1980
'Chrome-tin pink and red glazes', Stephanie Kalan, *Ceramic Review*, no. 47, 1977
'Lustred Earthenware', Sutton Taylor, *Ceramic Review*, no. 82, July/August 1982
Caiger-Smith, A., *Lustre Pottery*, London (Faber and Faber, 1985) (now in paperback – Herbert Press).

Techniques

The content of this chapter is chiefly related to my own workshop practice. Other tin-glaze potters may and do have different ways of doing things; where relevant, these differing procedures are explained in the individual profiles.

Preparation of the Glaze

Glazes containing a large proportion of non-clay materials such as frits tend to settle quite rapidly. An addition of 2% bentonite will help; this should be mixed in at the dry stage otherwise it will be difficult to absorb into the liquid glaze. If the biscuit has been high fired or the glaze is 'curtaining', the addition of a flocculant[1] may be necessary to give the glaze more bulk. Examples of flocculants are: Epsom salts (magnesium sulphate), calcium chloride, vinegar and gelatine. The flocculant should be added drop by drop until the desired viscosity is achieved. Gelatine needs to be dissolved in hot water first. The flocculating effect is only temporary. I find the addition of bentonite is sufficient for my purposes but the glaze does need regular stirring during the course of glazing.

The glaze should be mixed at least 24 hours before it is going to be used, sieved twice (60s and 100s mesh) and left to settle. The glaze is temporarily flocculated by the mixing activity and although it may appear thick enough to use, this appearance is usually deceptive and the glaze will actually fire too thin. If the glaze is left to settle, excess water can be skimmed off and the glaze thickness tested more accurately. A good idea of thickness can be gained from how much stays on a dipped hand, but a more accurate test can be made from dipping a small piece and then scratching the dried surface with a needle. Piccolpasso describes this same method and proclaims that the ideal thickness is that of 'the edge of one of those skins used for making gloves'! After using a particular glaze for some time, experience will tell you whether the thickness is correct or not.

Preparation of Pots for Glazing

It is worthwhile taking trouble to prepare a good, blemish-free surface for glazing and painting. After the biscuit firing, rough bits and flat bottoms of pots can be sanded down with medium-grade wet and dry paper. Then all bases and feet should be waxed with a hot mixture of candle wax and paraffin. Prior to glazing, the pots should be wiped well all over with a damp sponge. Alternatively, they can be dipped completely in water – in which case you need to wait half an hour or so until the colour begins to change before glazing. This process removes the sanding dust and helps the glaze to be fully absorbed into all the tiny air holes in the porous biscuit which otherwise would blow out after removing the pot from the glazing bin and leave pinholes in the glaze. Any pinholes that remain after glazing can be gently rubbed with a finger when dry.

Glazing

Pots should be glazed in order of size, starting with the smallest and thinnest-walled, which have lower absorbency and therefore need the

Dipping a large plate in glaze using tongs. *Photographs by Stephen Brayne. Courtesy of Ceramic Review.*

Lifting plate out of glaze using tongs with extra support from grip on footring.

thickest coating of glaze. Adjust the glaze by adding more water gradually as you move on to bigger pots. For an all-over coating, it is preferable to dip rather than spray the glaze* – with spraying it is difficult to gauge the thickness and it does not provide a good surface for painting. Pots should be dipped with tongs if possible – finger marks are always hard to touch up satisfactorily – in a large container. All of my bowls and dishes have a substantial waisted footring which can be gripped as the pot is brought out of the glaze bin. Tong scars can be rubbed over when dry.

I like to leave glazed pots for at least 24 hours before starting to decorate. A surface which has not completely hardened will be lifted off by the brush and will not absorb the pigments well. Pots can be left as long as you like. The important thing is to avoid too much rubbing and fettling which creates a powdery surface and impedes the flow of the brush. Bentonite in the glaze (see above) gives a good hard crust to the

* This applies to glazing when it is intended as an all-over base for maiolica painting. For different purposes, glazes can also be brushed, sprayed or poured, according to the desired effect.

glaze for easier painting. Liquid laundry starch can also be used for the same purpose. Two per cent SCMC (sodium carboxymethylcellulose) can be used as a glaze binder which increases hardness as well as adhesion and viscosity.

Sintering

This is a process whereby the glaze is fired to a point where a reaction has begun between the solids, causing the particles to stick together without melting taking place. Porosity is decreased and the strength of the surface increased. A sintered glaze provides a surface which is hard and yet still absorbs the pigments. Cardew[2] describes a method of calculating the sintering point of a glaze (known as the Tammann Temperature) which is approximately equivalent to 0.6 of the K (Kelvin) or absolute temperature of fusion. Thus, if the normal maturing temperature of a glaze is 1000°C, you must add on 273° (−273 is K zero or absolute zero) to arrive at a K or absolute temperature of 1273°. The glaze will therefore sinter at 0.6 of 1273°, which is 764°C. This temperature should be related to an appropriate cone. The sintered glaze surface is then decorated and refired to maturity. This is quite a time-consuming extra process. It is probably only necessary if very finely detailed decoration is being carried out, or if graded washes of colour are desired.

Brushes and Brushwork

It is vital to find brushes that accord with your vision. The choice of a brush ultimately depends either on what it will do for you or on what you want to do with it. Painting can be a real struggle with inappropriate brushes and a change of brush can make it all the more pleasurable. Looking at both historical and contemporary styles of painting on pots, they seem to separate out into two distinct ways of using the brush. The first is calligraphic in the sense that the content and manner of the painting is dictated by the quality of the brushstroke itself; the shape and character of the stroke is a main component of the design. Within this category falls much of the Islamic and Hispano-Moresque ware; Caiger-Smith's work is eminently calligraphic and I would also place in this category the painterly 'splash and streak' designs of for example Jane Gustin and Stanley Andersen. The other convention is generally more graphic in nature tending to use brushes more as fillers, shaders and liners in the service of a more pictorial vision. Italian maiolica and its offspring – French faience, Dutch and English delftware – are very

much at the source of this tradition; Gill, Ostrom and Manessi are good contemporary examples of this way of working.

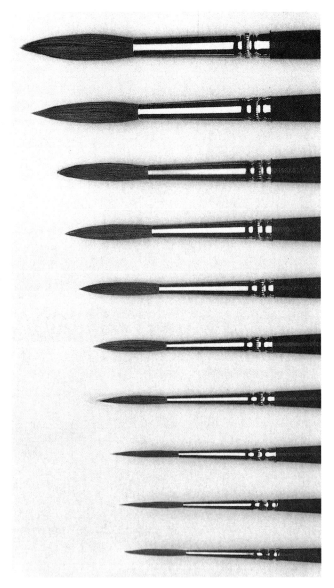

Pure red sable pointed writers (ticket writing brushes) *Courtesy A.S. Handover Ltd.*

Cipriano Piccolpasso, drawing, brush handle, thin brush and thick brush, from The Three Books of the Potter's Art, 1557. *Courtesy of the Board of Trustees of the Victoria and Albert Museum.*

Appropriate brushes could mean anything from decorators' paintbrushes to the finest sable! One important factor is their ability to hold colour. Stiff bristle brushes are generally too hard for this kind of surface. Watercolour brushes are more suitable. For my own work, I use nylon and sometimes sable watercolour brushes – one-strokes for large areas of colour, scriptliners or pointed writers for fine lines. They hold the colour well, have a good spring to them and last a long time. Other brushes worth trying are signwriting and ticket writing brushes mixed up an approximate ratio of 1 cup water/ 3 tablespoons gum-arabic powder. This mixture is then boiled and sieved – it should be the consistency of double cream – and kept in a brown glass jar in the dark (if kept in the light, it goes off very quickly). Glycerine is simply diluted in water before use. A solution of SCMC glaze binder (an organic cellulose gum) can also be used (mix 1–2 tablespoons per gallon of water and leave for 24 hours or follow supplier's instructions).

The Author's Painting Technique

Prior to painting, the bottoms of the pots are wiped clean of glaze and glaze dribbles or tong scars are fettled if necessary. All decorating is carried out on the electric wheel. Flatware is decorated on a large bat; tall pieces such as large jars and jugs are raised to eye level on bats and a banding wheel. Small pieces are held in the hand.

The design is first of all marked out roughly in soft pencil (3–6B). Then, starting with the palest pigments, areas of colour are filled in with various sizes of one-stroke watercolour brushes.

Pure red sable one-strokes (long)
Courtesy A.S. Handover Ltd.

and specialist wood-graining and marbling brushes. Chinese and Japanese brushes are suited to a more calligraphic orientation.

Painting Mediums

Although I do not do so myself, many potters add a painting medium to the pigments to improve the flow. Suitable mediums are gum-arabic and glycerine. The gum-arabic solution is

Filling in areas of colour – here ochrous yellow, red, green and pale blue

93

Outlining the areas in dark blue pigment. Here, in order to decorate the reverse, the plate is resting on bubble-wrap to prevent the glaze chipping off from the rim.

Painting the ground with strong blue pigment. Wax has been used to outline the shapes in order to give a clear-cut separation of dark ground from motifs.

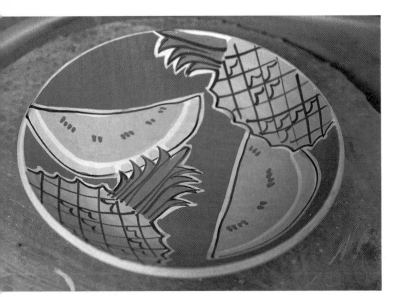

The completed plate ready for firing.

Detail of painting showing build up of colours on the apple. The texturing of the pigments is very pronounced here as the glaze is a little too thick (which has also caused crazing).
Photographs by Stephen Brayne, courtesy of Ceramic Review

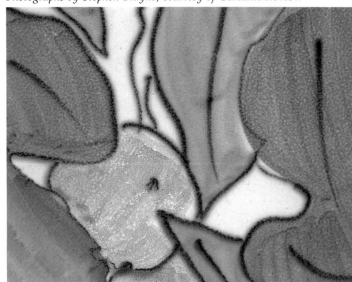

Sometimes areas are overpainted with darker or contrasting pigments to create depth or suggest volume; colours can be shaded in to each other with increasingly diluted pigments. For example, fruit shapes might have a pale yellow wash, overpainted with orange shading into green. A final colour might be red, shaded on over the orange. Examples of this technique can be seen on the apple in the photograph above, or on the pear on the back cover. When all the colour composition is complete, the whole is brought together and defined by a fine dark blue or blue-green outline. This is done using a scriptliner brush.

Cipriano Piccolpasso, drawing, potters painting their wares, from The Three Books of the Potter's Art, 1557.
Courtesy of the Board of Trustees of the Victoria and Albert Museum.

Newland used the technique only with a black glaze instead of the pigment (*cf.* Newland profile on p. 105).

Ifigenia Simonovic, teapot, 1985
Wax resist and painting with oxides and underglaze colours.
Private collection

Other Methods of Decoration

The pigments can of course be applied in a great variety of ways apart from painting – for example, sponging, spraying, stencils, stamps, screen printing etc. Sgraffito through the oxide to reveal a white line can be very effective for definition (as in the work of Matthias Ostermann, see p. 124).

Wax resist

This is a seductive technique, which can be used to create interesting layered and 'negative' effects. Hot wax (candle wax diluted with paraffin) forms the best resist, but it is messy and ruins the brushes quite quickly. The alternative is to use the cold wax emulsion resist although it is not so easy to apply.

Wax can also be used as a resist or as an etching surface for the stronger pigments on the leatherhard clay. The pigments harden on in the biscuit firing and will burn through the tin glaze.

Ann Clark, slipcast box, 15 cm, 1970s.
With wax resist and pigment on raw clay, later glazed with tin glaze at the biscuit stage.

95

Glaze on glaze

The use of transparent coloured glazes on top of the tin glaze gives a softer, more fluid effect than the straight pigments. The traditional Spanish techniques of *cuerda seca* (see photograph on p.23) and *cuenca* both made use of this method. The manganese-stained wax line of the former and the raised *cloisonné* walls of the second, in theory prevented the colours from running into one another. (In practice not always the case, as the large *cuerda seca* dishes were fired on their sides and the more fusible coloured glazes flowed over into adjoining sections.)

Another type of glaze on glaze technique is the Newland/Tower method of applying a contrasting coloured glaze over the fired tin glaze. This surface can then be used like a scraperboard for etching designs back to the white glaze (for a description of the technique, see Newland profile, p.102).

William Newland, test tile for a large mural, showing the cuenca technique of cloisonné walls separating the colours.
Photograph by Douglas Cape

Slips

Colour can also be created by the use of slips under the glaze. These are applied at the leather-hard stage. Pale coloured slips will be masked by the opaque glaze, but slips containing the stronger oxides of cobalt and copper will filter through the glaze to give a soft misty colour. The

copper slips come through quite turquoise in tone (see top photograph on p. 99). This technique is useful for creating a tinted background; it can also be used as another element in the decoration i.e. slip techniques of paper resist etc. can be used to create another layer of interest before decorating with in-glaze pigments (a technique used most effectively by Morgen Hall, see p.140).

Recipe suitable for use under a tin glaze:

Ball clay	70	
Nepheline syenite	20	
China clay	10	
Blue:	4%	cobalt oxide
Green:	6%	rutile
	2%	copper oxide
Green:	5%	copper carbonate
Grey-blue:	3%	nickel
	3%	iron chromate
	2%	cobalt oxide
Grey-green:	2½%	copper oxide
	3%	nickel
	½%	cobalt oxide

Sieve through 60s and 80s mesh. For better dispersion of cobalt in slips, sieve through 200s mesh, or use ready-milled cobalt.

On-glaze enamels

These were first used on Minai ware in 12th century Persia. In Europe in the 18th century, enamels were used extensively in France, Germany and Holland, in emulation of porcelain decoration. Enamels do not fuse with the glaze in the way that in-glaze pigments do. By remaining as a superimposed layer on top of the glaze, they always seem to emphasise the separateness of ornament. They can be used in combination with in-glaze pigments to create a contrasting layer of surface interest. This effect is exploited in the work of Lisa Katzenstein (see photograph on p.99). The firing range for enamels on earthenware glazes is in the 760–800°C range.

Firing

With the many higher firing red earthenware bodies available today, most potters opt for a low biscuit firing of 970–1000°C followed by a glaze firing in the 1060–1140°C range. It is quite feasible though to use the Continental method of a high bisque and low glost firing with its brighter colour range. With this last method, the bisque temperature obviously depends on the body used – it needs to be high enough to ensure a good glaze-body fit but not so high as to vitrify and make glazing difficult. Tests should be carried out to find the optimum temperature which would probably be within the 1040–1080°C range. Glost firing temperature could be anything from 950–1040°C. White earthenware bodies usually require a bisque of 1160–1190°C for a good glaze-body fit.

It is important in the biscuit firing to make sure that all the carbon and sulphur gases are burnt out. If the firing is too rapid, the gases remain trapped beneath the surface, only to cause pinholing or white spotting in the subsequent glaze firing (if it is higher in temperature). The burning-out process can be assisted by making sure the firing is taken slowly between 700 and 900°C – no more than 100° per hour. This is particularly advisable if flatware is stacked.

Tin or zirconium opacified glazes benefit from a slow firing particularly towards the upper limit, so that the glaze can mature gently, stabilise, and smooth over any pinholes in the surface. With a computer-controlled kiln, a slow firing and soak can be programmed – though it is advisable to double check with a cone to make sure the glaze is not being overfired. Manually-controlled kilns should be soaked in conjunction with observation of the cone. The aim is to retard the melting of the cone without actually losing temperature. A slow rate of climb for the last 100° combined with a minimum soak of one hour on the last cone would probably be sufficient for most glazes. Some old electric kilns fire so slowly that they induce a natural soak towards the end of the firing anyway!

Sometimes glazed wares need to be retouched, either with extra colour or glaze, and refired. Refires should never be to the same temperature as the original glaze firing as this is tantamount to overfiring and colours will run. Refiring to 2–3 cones below is usually adequate.

Troubleshooting

Common problems in tin-glazed earthenware:

Colours running

This could be due to a number of factors. The glaze could be too thickly applied or have 'curtained' when glazing (see p. 90). The glaze itself may be too fluxed for the firing temperature. In this case the glaze can be stiffened up either by reducing the flux content or by adding alumina and silica in the form of China clay (try 5–10% to start with). Alternatively, try firing the glaze a cone lower. It may be that the pigments are too concentrated (particularly applicable to cobalt and copper oxides) and need further dilution with China clay.

Colours rough and blistered

This is due to the refractoriness of certain pigments and stains (e.g. rutile, lemon yellow stain, some pale blue stains) in which case add more frit. Stronger oxides such as cobalt if applied too thickly will become oversaturated and rough to the touch. Dilute with China clay and/or frit.

Glaze crawling

Densely opacified white glazes are prone to crawling. This can happen if the glaze application is too thick and one can normally preempt the problem as the glaze on drying will crack like dried mud. In which case, wash off the glaze and start again. Some places like the angle where the handle joins the body collect the glaze which forms small cracks. Make sure these are luted over with a small wooden tool to prevent crawling in the glaze firing.

Glaze crazing

This is caused by a poor glaze-body fit and is most likely to happen if the clay body is underfired. If a low-expansion body, such as stoneware, white earthenware or buff, is not fired high enough in either the bisque or the glost firing, then in cooling it will not contract sufficiently to put the glaze under compression and prevent crazing. If any of these clays is used, either on their own or, as is often the case, mixed with red earthenware, then the bisque or glost firing temperature should be increased until crazing no longer occurs. As an example, a 50/50 mix of red and buff clays is craze resistant if taken to 1120°C. White earthenware usually requires a firing to at least 1160°C. If the tin glaze is highly alkaline (and therefore high-expansion), then it is also more prone to crazing. Small percentages of flint and borax can help. A glaze applied too thickly will also tend to craze. But otherwise, a tin glaze, being quite viscous because of its high opacity, is not normally susceptible to crazing, given that the body is correctly fired.

Glaze pinholing

This is usually caused by the bursting of gas bubbles through the glaze. If the glaze firing has been too rapid in the last stage, the holes do not have time to subside, nor does the glaze have time to heal over the craters. A slower, higher biscuit firing can also help. Pinholing can also occur on areas where the clay has been 'roughed up' by the turning process, creating little air pockets. Care must be taken when turning to smooth down the surface with a wooden tool, a finger or a metal kidney held flat. The dunking of pots in water prior to glazing (see p.90) will also counteract pinholing by aiding absorption of the glaze into all the air pockets.

Dunting

This can be a problem particularly with large plates and dishes which have turned feet. The stress on both expansion and contraction of such large flat areas is enormous. Care should be taken with firing and cooling slowly, particularly at the vulnerable temperatures of the quartz inversion (around 575°C) and the cristobalite 'squeeze' (around 225°C). Glaze thickness is crucial on these pieces. It tends to collect and be thicker at the bottom, exerting great pressure and causing the piece to split apart. Care should be taken when making such wares to create an even thickness throughout. Hollows and thin places will collect the glaze where the body is weakest, causing localised stresses and possible dunting cracks.

Toxicity

There is much concern these days about the safety of ceramic materials, both raw and fired. Harry Fraser[3] has pointed out that many household materials are also toxic and yet do not arouse the same degree of hysteria. If handled sensibly, observing basic principles of hygiene and caution (e.g. the wearing of a mask when preparing a glaze etc.), there is no reason why ceramic materials should give problems. Silica dust is the most hazardous substance to affect potters and it is important to try and minimise dust in the studio. Lead in its fritted forms of lead bisilicate and lead sesquisilicate is insoluble and therefore relatively harmless. Some of the most toxic materials are barium carbonate, antimony oxide, unfritted borax, manganese dioxide, nickel oxide and cadmium-based stains (some reds, yellows and oranges).

Metal release in glazes[4]

If glazes or stains containing either lead or cadmium are being used for domestic ware, it is important to make sure that the levels of metal release in the fired glaze are within the mandatory limits as set out below.

UK
Britain adopts British Standard (BS) 6748 with the following limits:

	Pb		Cd
Flatware (i.e. plates, saucers and dishes)	8	ppm*	0.7 ppm
Small holloware**	4	ppm	0.3 ppm
Large holloware (>3dm³)	1.5	ppm	0.3 ppm
Cookware	1.5	ppm	0.1 ppm

* parts per million
** Holloware is defined as 'any article in which the ratio of height to diameter is equal to, or exceeds, one half'.[5]

Opposite
Lisa Katzenstein, oval platters, 1991
Katzenstein's studio production pieces are slip-cast in white earthenware, bisque fired to 1160°C and then glazed with a leadless zirconium glaze, in-glaze painted and fired to 1060°C. The on-glaze motifs are applied in the form of transfers made from lino-cuts and fired at 800°C with a 20-minute soak.

Daphne Carnegy, plate (detail)
The green slip, applied at leatherhard stage, filters
through the tin glaze to give a softly tinted background
for the maiolica painting.

USA

The Food and Drugs Administration (FDA) introduced new release limits in September 1991:

	Pb		Cd	
Flatware	3	ppm	0.5	ppm
Small holloware	2	ppm	0.5	ppm
Large holloware ($>1.1\ dm^3$)	1	ppm	0.25	ppm
Jugs, cups, mugs	0.5	ppm	0.25	ppm

It is possible that Europe will eventually adopt these limits too. Furthermore it is likely that American limits will be periodically reduced to force the tableware industry unleaded.

The testing involves immersing ware in a 4% acetic acid solution at 20–25°C for 24 hours. This is followed by determination of the lead concentration in the solution using atomic absorption spectroscopy (AAS). With a general trend towards unleaded systems, there is an increasing demand for graphite AAS, where lead release can be detected down to 0.01 ppm. Addresses of testing stations are given below.

Metal release is affected by certain other factors:

1. Copper can weaken a lead-glass structure and introduce lead release values of up to 100x permissible levels. Avoid using copper on food contact surfaces. There is some research[6] indicating that the use of barium carbonate and chromium sesquioxide suppresses lead release in copper-bearing glazes.

2. A glaze containing a combination of lead and borax frits is less acid-resistant than one which is just based on lead bisilicate.

3. It is important that wares are fired to the correct temperature. Underfired glazes and pigments that are poorly glossed-over will be more susceptible to acid attack.

4. A higher silica content and higher glaze temperature will give a harder, more resistant glaze surface. Alumina and titania also assist in combating acid attack.

Metal release testing laboratories

UK

Testing Division
CERAM Research
British Ceramic Research Limited
Queens Road
Penkhull
Stoke-on-Trent ST4 7LQ
Tel: 0782 45431
(*lead, cadmium, zinc, antimony and specific food contact testing*)

USA

Cornell University
Ithaca, New York

Notes

1 Flocculants are acids or salts acting as acids, see Hamer, op. cit. for full explanation of their action.
2 Cardew, Michael, *Pioneer Pottery*, London (Longman, 1969)
3 Fraser, H., *Ceramic Faults and their Remedies*, London (A & C Black, 1986)
4 I am most grateful to Dr Philip Jackson of CERAM Research (British Ceramic Research Ltd) for his up-to-date information on the subject.
5 Fraser, op. cit.
6 Rodo, Paul W., *An Introduction to the Technology of Pottery*, 2nd Edition (Institute of Ceramics/Pergamon Press)

Opposite
Andrea Gill, detail of 'Vine Handle Vase', ht 75 cm, 1982.

SECTION III
Contemporary Perspectives

Individual Approaches

Tin-glazed Earthenware in the Studio Context

William Newland

'It wasn't that we were anti-Leach – but there were other things to do.'

William Newland's position in the history of tin glaze is of particular interest as it extends right through from the so-called 'Renaissance' period of craft pottery in the 1950s with its revival of the use of tin glaze, of which he was a prime instigator, up to the present day, where he is still actively and avidly engaged in the practice of maiolica.

His first contact with pottery was as a student at the Institute of Education in 1947. Originally from New Zealand, he had fought in the war, been taken prisoner in Germany, and on liberation, came to London to study painting at Chelsea. He discovered he had a natural flair for pottery and went on to attend Dora Billington's classes at the Central School. A year later, he found himself back at the Institute, this time as a teacher with a brief to 'do for pottery what Marion Richardson had done for painting and drawing'. This was an exciting time; spirits were beginning to lift after the war-time depression, energies were redirected into a new creative hothouse. The art schools were full of such artist teachers as Pasmore, who also experimented with ceramics, Moore and Sutherland. The Arts Council's exhibition in 1950 of Picasso's works had a tremendous impact; it became acceptable, desirable even for fine artists to turn their hand to ceramics. A stimulating atmosphere of cross-fertilisation was created between the previously quite separate worlds of Craft and the Fine Arts. The unself-conscious *joie-de-vivre* in Picasso's imagery led the way for a new lightheartedness

in British pottery – always a strong trait in the English artefact and in many ways a return to the sprightly mood of 17th century English delft-ware and slipware. The emphasis was very much on individual, one-off pieces – a reaction to the mass-production of utility ware in the austerity of the 1940s. Since his return from Japan in 1920, Bernard Leach had extensively and rather exclusively proselytised the oriental methods and traditions of high-fired stoneware

William Newland, tile, 22cm square, 1950.
A good example of the 'post-Picasso' face of the 1950s.
Photograph by Douglas Cape.

William Newland, large bowl 'Europa and the Bull', diam. 61cm, 1965.
This superb piece illustrates Newland's gestural style and his use of etched wax and wax resist.
Courtesy Christie's.

and his influence had dominated the pottery scene for many years. Dora Billington opened up other avenues and placed her faith in the emergence of a new contemporary, urban style. 'It wasn't that we were anti-Leach', says Newland, 'but there were other things to do.'

At the Institute, Newland was an inspirational teacher to a whole succession of students, all from a background of painting – James Tower, Nicholas Vergette and Margaret Hine among others not only learnt the technique of maiolica from him and adopted it as their chief medium of expression but also, under Newland's guidance, took it in a very new direction. In 1951, Newland, Hine and Vergette set up a studio together in Bayswater and shortly after had their first exhibition in a nightclub in Swallow Street. The fact that everything had to be displayed on the walls meant that they concentrated on making tile panels, bas-reliefs and murals. The show was a sell-out, and soon their work was to be seen decorating the interiors of restaurants and Italian-style coffee bars which were so much in vogue at the time. Alongside the architectural ceramics, they were also producing pots and figurative sculptural pieces – all derived from thrown forms. There was much experimentation and inventiveness and a new awareness of the thrown shape as 'something to work on'.

Newland's *Minoan Bull* and his wife Margaret Hine's *Pigeons* are characteristic figures, made from thrown and reassembled parts and with a vitality that would not be manifest in, say, a press-moulded object. Bowls were made and deftly cut into non-circular shapes (e.g. boat shape), ingeniously managing to retain the vigour of the original thrown shape. Dora Billington championed the new movement. In her article, 'The New Look in British Pottery' in *The Studio* (January 1955), she said, '. . . English studio pottery is at last acquiring a "New Look", more in tune with current ideas in house decoration and design generally. Gay, amusing, colourful – within the range of "good" pottery colour – an exciting mixture of sculpture, painting and potting.'

Newland's Own Approach to Pottery and Maiolica

Newland sees European pottery as separating roughly into two strains – one, deriving from Greek and Roman cultures, and moving up through Germany and Middle Europe, taking itself quite seriously, austere and 'hard', concerned with issues of truth to materials and conceptual, formal ideas. Here would be placed such artists as Rie, Coper, Auld and Lowndes.

Margaret Hine, Pigeon, ht 23cm, 1950.
Thrown and assembled. Etched black glaze overfired tin glaze (see p. 105).
Photograph by Douglas Cape

William Newland, oxide sketches on biscuit.
Photograph by Douglas Cape

William Newland, tests for 'Europa and the Bull' showing use of black glaze under tin glaze.
Photograph by Douglas Cape

The other, originating in Manises and developing in such countries as Portugal, Holland and England, is expressive of a much more lighthearted approach to life, more modest in its aims, often of a simple utilitarian and decorative nature, the surface lending itself more easily to illustration, humour and pastiche. This strain would naturally include much of European slip and tin-glaze ware as well as the ceramics of Picasso, Matisse and Lurçat.

Newland places himself firmly in the *joie-de-vivre* strain, describing himself as a primitive and a country boy at heart. His New Zealand farm boyhood formed the foundation for his interest in animal subjects; through these, the maximum power of expression is sought through the quality of the line. The idea of gestural drawing, of 'feeling in the line', is a driving force in Newland's work. For him, this approach is exemplified in Chinese brushwork, the drawings of Michelangelo and Rembrandt; in ceramics by some of the Dutch tile painters and the calligraphic style of Hispano-Moresque decoration. He works both in slipware and maiolica, some forms of expression being more suitable to one medium than the other. He tends to work on a series of pots, dealing with variations on a theme. Recent tin-glaze work includes large bowls portraying Europa and the Bull.

The wheel is an important tool for Newland. He describes himself as a 'touch' person, who took to throwing with astonishing ease. His large pieces have all the spring and vigour of the experienced and confident thrower. Some pieces are also press-moulded. He is also still very much involved with the world of architectural ceramics, producing panels, sculptures and reliefs on a large scale.

Technical Information

Newland has always been highly experimental in an empirical way, constantly on the look out for new ways of doing things. The *cuenca* tiles of Toledo with their raised *cloisonné* effect engendered a similar use of coloured tin glazes. Similarly the Florentine 'oak-leaf' jars and jugs with their relief blue glaze on top of the tin glaze gave rise to glaze-on-glaze experiments. He taught James Tower the following technique:

Glaze the article all over with a white (tin) glaze and fire. Heat the pot up to 100°C and apply a black glaze (containing approximately 1 oz sugar for every kilo of glaze, for good adhesion) to the fired surface. It is then possible to scratch or scrape through the black glaze to reveal the white underlying glaze.

A technique much used by Newland and his contemporaries starts with a design etched into wax-coated leatherhard clay. A black glaze suitable for raw firing is then applied to the etched areas. After the object has been bisque fired, a white tin glaze is applied over the whole surface. In-glaze pigments can also be applied at this stage. In the subsequent glaze firing, the black glaze burns through the tin glaze to give a soft textured brown not dissimilar to the soft manganese purple brown of English delftware.

Traditional maiolica glaze (Kenneth Clark for Dora Billington)

60	Litharge
40	Cornish stone
20	Tin oxide

Seger molecular formula:

PbO	0.8	Al_2O_3	0.2	SiO_2	1.68
K_2O	0.09			SnO_2	0.46
Na_2O	0.06				
CaO	0.05				

Probably not suitable for ordinary domestic use because of its high lead content. Firing temperature 1080–1100°C. Good on red clay. Has 'the fatty quality of Lambeth bellarmines'.

Black Glaze

75	Lead bisilicate
25	Ball clay
10	Manganese dioxide

Alan Caiger-Smith

Acknowledged and respected worldwide both as a skilled practitioner and an authority on all aspects of the subject, be they technical, historical or philosophical, Alan Caiger-Smith has been making tin-glazed earthenware since 1955 when he established the pottery workshop at Aldermaston. Pottery at the time was mostly austere and lacking in colour, dominated by either the browns and creams of traditional English slipware, the rich but subtle tones of oriental-inspired stoneware, popularised by the work of Bernard Leach, or the uncompromising formal concerns of Rie and Coper. Maiolica was considered an indulgence, its ornament superficial. Caiger-Smith had studied painting at Camberwell before going on to read History and English at Cambridge, where in his spare time, he was already experimenting with clay modelling and pottery. A visit to Spanish tin-glaze potteries in Triana, Seville in 1952 gave him the impetus to take up pottery in a more serious way and he then went on to study ceramics at the Central School under Dora Billington, Gilbert Harding-Green and Kenneth Clark. With the encouragement of Billington, he chose tin glaze as his means of expression; one which would give him maximum potential for painted decoration and bright colours. Interestingly, he also recalls a childhood experience of delight in washing up a faience plate from Quimper which was so bright and colourful amongst the plain utility crockery of the wartime household.

So, with an aim to produce domestic pottery which would also please the eye, both in use and out of it, Caiger-Smith set up the Aldermaston Pottery. In these days of the individual studio potter, it is surprising to find such an establishment, probably also inspired by the Spanish potteries, where pots are produced in fairly large quantities by a team of workers. It soon becomes evident though, that this is not the traditional country pottery with strict division of labour and that it operates on a very different basis. On entering the workshop, there is an immediate feeling of cooperative effort, and although there is very much a house style emanating from Caiger-Smith's distinctive designs, each person is allowed maximum freedom within this parameter to contribute to all

stages of production of the standard wares and eventually to make their own designs as well. New techniques, ideas and designs can be devised by any member of the team and some are assimilated into the working pattern of the Pottery. It is very much a mutual teaching and learning environment. Approximately eight people are employed there, all at varying levels of competence and experience, ranging from Edgar Camden, a mainstay of the establishment, who has been there since 1961, to college leavers who come to gain valuable insight into workshop practice. The wood firings perhaps best embody the cooperative spirit of the workshop; participation in the transformation process is a significant and unifying experience for all concerned. The human element is all-important in a small workshop like this, where production is labour-intensive and a high standard of craftsmanship is regarded as more important than

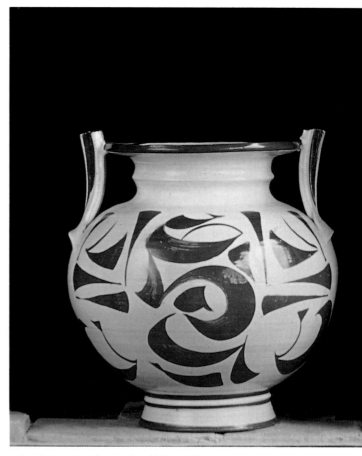

Alan Caiger-Smith, two-handled pot, ht 56 cm, 1992.
Reduced silver-copper lustre on tin glaze.
Collection Pearl Assurance plc. Photograph by Julian Bellmont.

Alan Caiger-Smith, bowl, diam. 46cm, 1992.
Silver-copper blend of reduced-pigment lustre on tin glaze.
Photograph by Marcus Lyon.

money-spinning mass production *per se*. A fine balance is sought between maintaining enough flexibility to allow for innovation and creative development whilst stressing the importance of repetitive work for understanding of both form and decoration, and for fluency and viability – a situation peculiar to the small production workshop. With regard to decoration, the emphasis is quite naturally on the development and transmission of a shareable language rather than on a more individualistic approach.

Caiger-Smith's own work is, by his own defi-

nition, primarily concerned with 'formalised movement and abstraction'. Although he occasionally does decorate in a figurative manner, he is trying to get right away from the pictorial 'space-box' convention so closely linked with the tin-glaze tradition, which ignored or contradicted the three-dimensional elements of the pot, and which used the brush more as a

107

pencil and a filler-in of outlines than for its inherent capabilities. For Caiger-Smith, the starting points are colour and the power of the brush. He spent years learning the language of each type of brush, finding out what each was capable of. Some ideas for decoration were impossible to carry out on the pot because they were not sympathetic to the expressions of the brush. As with the Spanish pots whose generosity and energy first excited his interest in tin glaze, he is striving for an endlessly exciting and rhythmic 'dance' by means of an open-ended abstract calligraphic language. Reference is made to T.S. Eliot's 'still point in the turning world' as an ideal. Decoration is seen as an exploration of form, just as 'bare feet discover the sand'. After many years of trying to 'follow the form' as he had been taught in his classes, came the gradual realisation that decoration really begins at the form-making stage and 'demands a particular kind of attention, not only to the shape and surface texture of the main areas where the brush will work but also to details of rim and lip and especially to any pronounced changes in the profile' ('Why Decorate Pots', *Crafts*, Sept/Oct 1981). 'Some forms don't want to be painted.' By contrast, Caiger-Smith cites the example of the albarello as one which has remained so long in the tradition of decorated pottery because of its particular ability to invite ornament. Whatever is painted on a form cannot alter the form but can alter the way it is seen, can give different emphases, evoke a multitude of images. A sense of symbol, beyond mere ornament, is important; for Caiger-Smith, 'good decoration goes far beyond the appeal to the eye. It has much in common with the language of dreams and magic . . . relating to a world we do not really understand but are constantly exploring.'

One of the main attractions of the medium of tin glaze for Caiger-Smith is the transformation of the pigments in the firing and, with it the success or failure of the design – the fusion of the colours with the glaze, the way some colours retain their definition, others become soft and volatile; some lines 'weep' with the movement of the underlying glaze; different textures develop – some matt, some grainy, some characteristically dappled with white spots where the glaze has broken through the pigment.

Caiger-Smith's personal preferences in the history of tin glaze – Islamic and particularly Hispano-Moresque ware – are manifest in his work by way of underlying but well-assimilated references. There are reminders in the calligraphic style, in some of the shapes – the albarellos for example, and, not least, in the use of reduced lustre on-glaze decoration, which is carried out alongside, and sometimes in combination with the in-glaze decoration. In fact, the main body of Caiger-Smith's personal work is now primarily concerned with the use of lustres.

Processes and Techniques

The clay body used is Fremington clay, fetched raw from the pit. Nine tonnes last approximately one year. The clay is first of all dried out. It is then blended in a blunger with water and 7% dolomite is added, which stabilises this very fusible clay and increases the firing range, thereby reducing the risk of bloating. (Fremington clay usually begins to melt quite dramatically round about 1080°C.) On exit from the blunger, the slip is screened through a 30s, 40s, and 60s mesh sieve before sinking into a tank. It is kept in suspension in the tank by a revolving paddle. It is then sucked up into a filter press which renders it the right consistency for use.

Alan Caiger-Smith, bowl on deep foot, diam. 33 cm, 1992. Silver-copper reduced-pigment lustre. Photograph by Marcus Lyon.

Alan Caiger-Smith, bottle with plume handle, ht 25.5 cm, 1992. Black and grey in-glaze painting with chestnut lines. Photograph by Marcus Lyon.

and cross-draft system. The firing is so smooth that the usual problems of fly ash, flame and reduction smoke, necessitating the use of saggars to protect the tin glaze from blemishes and blistering, are virtually eliminated. Saggars are only used right next to the bagwall where the flame is fiercest. There are three stoke-holes and facilities for both primary and secondary air. Propane gas is often used to start the firings, and wood is used from 600°C. The wood used is willow, making use of the rejects from the local cricket bat willows. Caiger-Smith finds truth in Piccolpasso's claim that willow (and poplar) are the best woods for maiolica firings, giving a long soft flame, as opposed to the shorter, fiercer flame of hardwoods. A glaze firing takes about 14–15 hours. A slow, gentle firing, with its slight mixture of oxidation and reduction, gives not only better distribution of heat but also a generous, fat quality to the glaze and a particular development to the colours, not obtainable in a totally oxidised atmosphere.

A wide variety of pigments is used including both oxides and commercial underglaze colours. Where possible he prefers to use the oxides undiluted so that there is greater sensitivity to thickness of application, but sometimes about 10% flux (preferably alkaline) is added to the more refractory pigments. The colours are ground with water on a tile using a palette knife.

Most of the pots are thrown. Exceptions are large press-moulded dishes, and mugs and certain small bowls and plates whose shapes are more reliably repeated in quantity by jigger and jolley.

In traditional Continental fashion, the pots are given a high bisque firing – 1060°C. The subsequent glaze firing is only to 1040°C. The reason for this procedure is twofold: the high bisque gives a stronger, more craze-proof, less porous body, and the lower glaze firing means that the maximum range of bright colours is still attainable.

The main kiln used (for bisque, glost and lustre firings) is a 160 cubic foot wood-fired kiln, built to Caiger-Smith's own design 28 years ago, and it is still, despite constant use, in pristine condition today. He had found that a catenary arch downdraft kiln produced too much reduction and too much turbulence at the top, so he devised this kiln with its semi-circular vault

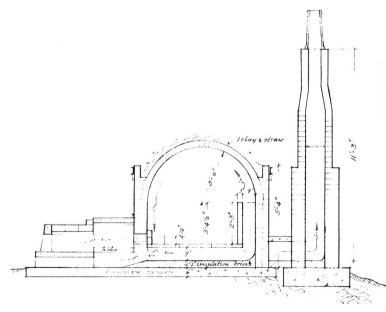

Diagram showing section of Alan Caiger-Smith's cross-draught wood-firing kiln. *Drawing by Anne-Marie Caiger-Smith.*

109

A little gum arabic (previously mixed with hot water) is added to improve the flow of the mixture. The pigments are then used like water colours.

Brushes used include Japanese brushes and a variety of signwriters' brushes made from ox and sable. A Dylon blue dye is sometimes used to sketch out designs (both for in-glaze and on-glaze decoration) prior to application of the pigments. For wax-resist techniques, cold wax emulsion is used in preference to hot wax as the latter quickly ruins brushes.

GLAZE RECIPES (all 1020–1060°C, oxidation or wood fired with intermittent reduction)

057 Glaze

Lead bisilicate	62
China clay	5
Cornish stone	11
Borax frit (P2955)	10
Zinc oxide	2
Tin oxide	10

Seger molecular formula:

PbO	0.70	Al_2O_3	0.22	SiO_2	2.24
KNaO	0.10	B_2O_3	0.09	SnO_2	0.26
CaO	0.10				
ZnO	0.10				

A general purpose, white glaze with a good colour range.

T4/91 Glaze

Lead sesquisilicate	77
China clay	16
Flint	7
Tin oxide	10

Seger molecular formula:

PbO	1.00	Al_2O_3	0.26	SiO_2	2.56
				TiO_2	0.13
				SnO_2	0.28

A warmer white capable of giving rich iron-browns, especially in wood-fired conditions.

Barium Matt Glaze

Lead bisilicate frit (P2950)	53
China clay	2
Cornish stone	12
Borax frit (P2955)	9
Barium carbonate	9
Flint	5
Tin oxide	10

Seger molecular formula:

PbO	0.62	Al_2O_3	0.18	SiO_2	2.37
KNaO	0.10	B_2O_3	0.08	SnO_2	0.27
CaO	0.10				
BaO	0.18				

Best in intermittent reduction in wood-firing. Gives a wide range of gentle colours.

Zinc Matt Glaze

Lead bisilicate frit (P2950)	56
Borax frit (P2955)	8
Cornish stone	10
Zinc oxide	8
China clay	4
Talc	4
Tin oxide	10

Seger molecular formula:

PbO	0.48	Al_2O_3	0.15	SiO_2	1.64
K_2O	0.02	B_2O_3	0.06	SnO_2	0.20
Na_2O	0.04				
CaO	0.07				
MgO	0.09				
ZnO	0.29				

W/A Glaze

Lead bisilicate (P2950)	28
*F borax frit	40
Zinc oxide	4
China clay	3
Flint	6
Zirconium silicate	9
Barium carbonate	1
Tin oxide	9

* An old Podmore frit, now made to special order. A medium-hard borax frit (e.g. Potterycrafts 2955) could possibly be substituted, although thorough testing should be carried out before changing the glaze as a lustre-base.

Seger molecular formula:

PbO	0.29	Al_2O_3	0.15	SiO_2	2.12
Na_2O	0.19	B_2O_3	0.33	SnO_2	0.21
CaO	0.33			ZrO_2	0.17
BaO	0.02				
ZnO	0.17				

110

A dense fat white, giving good blue-greens, but otherwise limited colour range. It has a low softening point and can be used for reduced lustre firings.

Pigments

Below are some examples of percentage pigment mixtures used at Aldermaston.

They are very concentrated and can be diluted if desired with clear alkaline or lead glaze. Many also benefit from the addition of a little China clay or red clay.

Cobalt Blues

Cobalt oxide	50
Tin glaze or clear glaze	50
Cobalt oxide	75
Ilmenite	25
Cobalt oxide	30
Ferric oxide	70
Cobalt oxide	84
Copper oxide	8
China clay	8

Alan Caiger-Smith, dish, diam. 36 cm, 1992.
Tin-glaze. Painted with in-glaze cobalt-silver pigment, over resist, and later painted with copper and silver pigments and fired in reduced lustre kiln.
Photograph by Marcus Lyon.

Iron Colours

Ferric oxide	87
Copper oxide	13
Ferric oxide	80
Manganese dioxide	10
Copper oxide	10

(A black for oxidation only)

Ferric oxide	33
Cobalt oxide	33
Chromium oxide	20
Clear glaze	14

Blue-Greens

Copper oxide	75
Cobalt oxide	25
Copper oxide	46
Ilmenite	39
Cobalt oxide	15

Orange-brown

Underglaze orange	95
Manganese dioxide	5

Purple

Chrome-tin-red stain	86
Whiting	9
Cobalt oxide	5

Grey

Manganese dioxide	60
Copper oxide	40

All mixtures give the best effect if they are finely ground.

Reduced-Pigment Lustre

The glazes used as a base for reduced lustres differ from the glazes used for in-glaze work in that they have a lower softening point to facilitate the formation of the lustre. They generally have a high sodium content which gives a better bonding of lustre to glaze. The glaze W/A given above softens at about 660°C and is capable of giving good lustres. Caiger-Smith uses several glazes in order to make use of the variation of temperature in the kiln and also to promote different colour responses.

Lustres are applied to the previously glazed ware and necessitate a third firing with a reduction atmosphere. Sometimes in-glaze painting has been carried out which in turn will be affected by the reduction atmosphere of the lustre firing – notably copper mixtures.

Compounds of silver and copper are mixed with red ochre (yellow ochre being too fusible) in an approximate 30%/70% ratio. The copper mixtures give better results if they are first calcined and ground. The mixtures are applied rather like a slip – painted, sprayed or sponged – to the glazed surface. In contrast to working on the unfired glaze, when painting on a fired glaze surface, the brush encounters no resistance and the movement of the brush is considerably extended.

The lustre firing requires an airy pack and takes 6½–7 hours to reach a temperature of approximately 660–670°C. When the glaze begins to soften very slightly (judged by removing draw rings), the atmosphere in the kiln is strongly reduced followed by periods of alternating oxidation (to keep the temperature up) and reduction. The length of this procedure is dependent on the size of the kiln and the intensity of the reduction.

If the firing temperature and the type of reduction have been appropriate, the ochre (which has protected the metals from re-oxidising) can be rubbed off with a cloth and fine grog, thereby revealing the lustres which result from the reduction of the pigments to the state of pure metals.

Examples of lustre pigments

Silver carbonate	20
Red clay or ochre	80
(silvery-amber-gold)	
Copper sulphide	27
Silver sulphide	7
Red clay or ochre	66
(orange gold to red)	

All pigments should be finely ground for optimum results.

There is a much more comprehensive discussion of lustreware techniques in Caiger-Smith's own book, *Lustre Pottery* (see Bibliography on p. 172).

Andrea Gill

A key figure in the recent revival of interest in maiolica in North America, Andrea Gill gave validation to it as a studio practice and she has been inspirational and encouraging to many potters turning to this technique. Trained as a painter, she went on to study ceramics at Alfred University, where she now teaches. A visit to Italy introduced her to the technique. She was further encouraged in the pursuit of earthenware through her contacts at Alfred with John Gill, Betty Woodman and Wayne Higby. She works in both slipware and maiolica.

My interest has been in the area of the relationship between surface and form within the formal structure of a pot. Most of my work is fairly large scale (two to three feet for vases, bowls about a foot deep and a foot and a a half across). The forms are traditional in stance – that is, how they sit on the table – but the relationship between the form and surface are less tied to tradition.

Physically and visually, the maiolica glaze does not become a part of the structure of the clay. It remains very much a loose skin on the surface, having a very different quality from the melting of stoneware glazes on high-fire clay. I believe that this separation is one reason why so much low-fire work is involved with surface; the glaze, unlike the stoneware glaze, remains above the form, creating a shaped canvas for further exploration. (*Studio Potter*, vol 11, no 2, 'In the Beginning was Earthenware')

The glaze seems to take on a form of its own . . . like clothes on a body. Like clothes, the glaze also offers the opportunity to deal with color and pattern in ways that can profoundly affect the way that the form is perceived. I think that pattern is not mindless, that it informs about (creates) space on a surface, can have meaning that is magical, narrative or contemplative. These aspects are only perceived gradually, as the surface must first relate to the form.

Maiolica for Gill is a satisfactory compromise between the stoneware integration of glaze and body and the superficial look of china painting – which retains the appearance of paint. The fusion of colours into glaze in maiolica gives a softness not found in other ceramic techniques.

I'm trying to make the form and the decoration completely dependent upon each other, so the form suggests things that can happen on the surface and the surface suggests forms that may relate to other forms. Sometimes I'm interested in camouflaging the form with patterns all over so it almost nullifies all the things that are happening to the form. I like people to see things in my work that look like other things. I like playing with things people can relate to without being too specific, like figures. (From *Low-fire Ceramics* by Susan Wechsler)

This element of playing with space, of illusion, pastiche and irony, is a reinterpretation of a type of imagery that has always been associated, from the Italian Renaissance onwards, with tin-glazed earthenware.

. . . I happened to wander into the ceramic section of the museum in Barcelona, and I think the pots there really affected me. As I remember, they were much looser than the Italian work, much closer to folk art than the Renaissance painting. I think that most ceramicists are working off this tradition in much the same way that medieval pottery has affected the stoneware in the Leach tradition. Although I still respond to the lively simplicity of the useful ware, I think my work has more in common with the painting emphasis of the Italian ware. I found in looking at the Italian pots, that they were much more concerned with creating a picture plane and depicting real space as opposed to patterning in the Spanish tradition. Even the early Orvieto ware was more concerned with using line to describe a real situation than the Spanish ware of the same period.

Andrea Gill, 'Ravenna Vase', ht 61cm, 1989.
Photograph by Stephen Myers.

Andrea Gill, 'Marie's Madonna', ht 71cm, 1990.

113

Although Gill's approach has more in common with the self-conscious illusionism of High Renaissance maiolica, her direct, rather naive style of painting still retains links with the folk art strain of the tradition.

Gill's work contains constant references to other ceramics, other art forms. The 'pot on a pot' is a much explored theme. Winged containers suggest ancient connotations. Figures have echoes of Romanesque statuary. Flower, leaf and vine motifs hark back to old decorative conventions. These patterns are juxtaposed and used to jump out from or fade back into the surface.

Making pots is still the only valid framework for Gill:

> If they weren't (pots), the forms might not make sense. I think I'm trying to stay close to what pottery is about, to stay within the framework of vessels and yet say that pottery doesn't have to be functional to be valid. When you look at the history of ceramics, most of it wasn't functional – ceramics has always been a middle class art. . . . If you couldn't afford a big hunting scene for the wall, you had it on a maiolica plate. (*Low-fire Ceramics*)

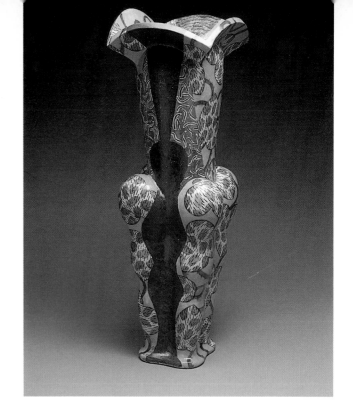

Andrea Gill, 'Undulating Vase', ht 69cm, 1991.
Photograph by Evelyn Snyder

Opposite
Andrea Gill, large vase, ht 61cm, 1988.
Photograph by Stephen Myers

Below
Andrea Gill, 'Demeter', 46cm x 38cm, ht 24cm, 1991.
Photograph by Lee Rexrode

Observations on Processes

Gill has found that it is better for her to separate the forming process and the painting process. She works on the wet clay with little plan for the painted surface.

The pots are slab-built, using press-moulds for parts. Gill sees the pot as a line, presenting endless possibilities for playing with space. The use of press-moulds permits shapes to be reproduced, thus providing the opportunity to try out different 'solutions' to the same contour.

Once I have a group of bisque pieces, I draw them, work out possible surface solutions in sketches, and then draw on the pot in pencil to figure out what will really work. Of course the maiolica has to be more planned than the slip work, as lighter colors do not cover darker ones, and overlaying colors sometimes gives very disappointing results.

I sometimes use wax stencil paper to apply the patterns. This gives a different line quality of edge to the color (slightly darker outline). Sometimes I use the stencils as a guide, sketching in the pattern with a pencil. . . . It is difficult to use the stencils on very convex shapes or in tight corners.

My work is not functional and the technical part of my work could stand some improvement (crazing, pinholing, crawling, color palette, color texture . . .) but I wonder if I really want a perfect product. I love the *istoriata* plates that have pieces of the deco crawling away from the rim . . . material getting the last say on this otherwise perfectly correct object.

Andrea Gill, 'Embrace', 50cm x 35cm, ht 25cm, 1990. Lent by The Hand and the Spirit/Joanne Rapp Gallery, Scottsdale, Arizona. Photograph by Craig Smith.

Technical notes

Bisque and glaze temperature: Orton Cone 06.

Clay body

Cedar Heights Redart	60
Fire clay	20
Ball clay	10
Talc	10
Fine grog	10

Barium carbonate: ¼ cup per 100lb dry.

Glaze Recipes (Cone 06–04)

Batz Glaze (04)

Ferro frit 3124	100
China clay	15
Barium carbonate	4
Zircopax or Zircosil 5	24

½% golden brown stain optional.

Seger molecular formula:
(approximate)

KNaO	0.34	Al_2O_3	0.31	SiO_2	2.42
CaO	0.61	B_2O_3	0.60	ZrO_2	0.34
BaO	0.05				

Greg's Revision

Ferro frit 3124	76.1
Barium carbonate	3.0
Edgar Plastic Kaolin (EPK) (China clay)	15.2
Calcined kaolin	5.7
Zircopax or Zircosil 5	11.7–13.7

Add ½% rutile to make off-white.

Seger molecular formula:
(approximate)

KNaO	0.34	Al_2O_3	0.43	SiO_2	2.57
CaO	0.61	B_2O_3	0.60	ZrO_2	0.23
BaO	0.05				

AG3

Ferro frit 3124	66
Ferro frit 3292	8
Whiting	5.6
Kona F-4 felspar (Soda felspar)	9.4
Edgar Plastic Kaolin (EPK) (China clay)	11
Zircopax or Zircosil 5	14

D.K.

Ferro frit 3124	40
Ferro frit 3292	40
Whiting	8
Edgar Plastic Kaolin (EPK) (China clay)	9
Flint	3
Zircopax	13

Base 1

Ferro frit 3124	77
Whiting	7
Kona F4 felspar (Soda felspar)	14
Edgar Plastic Kaolin (EPK) (China clay)	2
Zircopax or Zircosil 5	15
Bentonite	1
Epsom salts	0.2
Liquid laundry starch	1 tsp

Seger molecular formula:
(approximate)

K_2O	0.01	Al_2O_3	0.22	SiO_2	2.13
NaO	0.32	B_2O_3	0.48	ZrO_2	0.22
CaO	0.67				

Colourants

60	Mason's flux 6908
40	glaze stains

(Amount of flux and water needed vary according to stain)

Liquid laundry starch (1 tbsp. per 100 g) is added for hardness and glycerin (about 1 tsp. per 100 g) for flow.

Mix with water and about 1 tbsp. per gallon of muriatic acid to help prevent settling.

Alan Peascod

Translations and Iconoclasm

Alan Peascod's career has been marked by an intensity and breadth of research, both historical and technical, which has been the foundation for his energetic pursuit of new approaches to both form and surface treatment. His main areas of focus have been tin-glazed lustreware and dry-glaze surfaces. The world of Islam in particular has provided a basis for this research and been a powerful stimulus for the creation of a very personal vocabulary.

At the outset of his career, Peascod was making domestic stoneware in the Leach-Anglo-Japanese tradition. He has always valued this experience because he feels it developed his sensibility to clay and, although he himself was soon to look to other cultural traditions, it gave him a sense of the importance of an aesthetic and philosophical framework, the conviction that a pot must have 'more than what it is wearing'. From the early 1970s onwards, Alan has travelled extensively in Iran, Iraq, Egypt, Turkey and Europe studying and photographing museum collections and absorbing techniques, processes and attitudes. His deep interest in images and image-making on ceramics generated much of the research activity; his encounters with practising potters and his long-standing friendship with Alan Caiger-Smith further strengthened his commitment to the decorated image. Although he no longer makes domestic ware as such, he is still very preoccupied with the vessel and refers to his pots as 'the product of a deep love of the container form'. Much of his innovative experimentation with glazes and firing techniques has found application and confirmation in his teaching, which has been inspirational to a whole generation of Australian students.

In the recent dry-surface work, there is an exploration of new ideas in a deliberate attempt to translate the maiolica principle to a new format or mode of expression. The images used by Peascod have their source and inspiration in traditional tin glaze in the sense that he endeavours to devise clearly executed images which have a highly symbolic or referential content. The glaze tonality – white as a background in combination with terracotta, red or black colours – is an intentional reference to the maiolica strategy. Only in the dry matt surfaces does the work depart totally from traditional methods.

Alan Peascod, Jug Form, ht 42cm, 1989.
Reduced silver/copper lustre fired with cypress pine in purpose-built wood-firing kiln. Tin glaze fired to 1080°C.

I originally developed an affinity with maiolica whilst researching tin-glazed lustrewares in Italy, Spain and the Middle East. I feel that maiolica wares possess unique ceramic qualities (that is, surfaces that have an optical, three-dimensional depth) whilst providing one of the greater opportunities to explore the world of the painted image. As a teacher I find maiolica and slip methods are very useful tools to induce the pottery student into coming to terms with the essential skill of drawing. This is turn helps the student to realise that the painted image has the power to lift pottery expression into the world of social context. By producing images, stories can be evolved which add a sense of mystery and cultural purpose and may reflect the historical events or attitudes of any particular time.

Having said this, I feel that not *all* maiolica ceramics – contemporary or historical – are necessarily successful. To me a good pot is a harmonious integration of image, surface

Alan Peascod, Jar Form, ht 35cm, 1991.
Wood-fired reduced silver/copper lustre, on tin/zirconium opacified lead glaze.

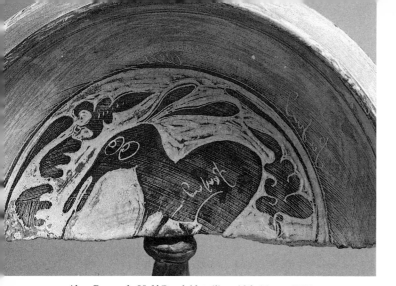

Alan Peascod, Half Bowl (detail), width 32cm, 1991.
Dry titanium white, brush decoration, gas fired several
times to approximately 1150°C.

area, surface type and three-dimensional
form.

Whilst I also think that cultural appropria-
tion is within reason acceptable, I also feel
there is an implied responsibility for potters
and ceramic artists to extend the content and
skill in their work beyond any previous artistic attempts. Having explored traditional
colour stain maiolica, I realised that the format was not appropriate to my own particular expression. I began to analyse the more
abstracted ideas surrounding the colour/
white background relationship. I began to develop dry matt glaze types based on barium,
titanium, tin and zircon silicates, to be used
with a range of warm earth colours ranging
from terracotta to black. The limiting of the
colour choice was deliberate as I found many
of the commercial stains too raw for my purposes. When I do use stains, I make my own
as I prefer the softer and slightly impure
colours the less refined studio methods
produce.

The glazes are fired to between 960°C and
1160°C in oxidised or reduced atmospheres. In
all cases the bisque firing is to 1200°C – often
in a reducing atmosphere. This may sound
slightly contradictory but in fact Australian
terracotta clays are quite refractory compared
to their English counterparts. I prefer density
and vitrification in my work. The pieces are
fired several times over. In each case re-
glazing may occur as well as surface re-
painting. The fired surfaces are quite tough

and this enables me to grind the surfaces by
hand to bring up the fine details in the
images.

The images I use were originally highly
abstracted spin-offs from early Islamic organic
designs. More recent work has concentrated
on figurative images expanding the theme of
human behaviour within the institutionalised
context.

Peascod has a healthy disregard for conventional ceramic protocol:

The working approach I have evolved is entirely self-centred and a response to my own
deep-rooted suspicion of everything I had
been taught or read and is the result of a total
incomprehension of Seger formulation and
anything else relying on intellectual rather
than intuitive process. . . .

By nature I am impatient . . . pushing the
ceramic medium to the limit until it finally
tells me to back off – it doesn't like it – and we
compromise. I force my work dry from the
wet to the point of destruction; pack and fire
my work to the point of irreverence (a 2–3
hour firing is the norm) and unpack the results at temperatures which are screaming at
you to go away and have a beer or something.
. . .

. . . I like to think of myself as a closet iconoc-
last and dry glaze methodology certainly
assists these ambitions. The demands of the
discipline are almost diametrically opposed to
standard, accepted conventions of body, glaze
and firing resolutions. I find the technique as
perverse and hence, as enticing, as lustre
technology. Increasingly these days my main
work objective is assiduously to preserve the
connection point between idea and finished
product. If work process becomes protracted
and out of phase with thought process I find I
run the risk of my mind slipping into neutral
gear, reducing the original idea to a whimper.
Despite the temptation to succumb to the trap
of describing the pitting of one's wits against a
glaze or firing procedure, I feel that these
notions are largely irrelevant. . . . Ultimately
the successful work must express itself per-
sistently and irrevocably. (*Ceramic Review*, No.
93, May/June 1985)

Tin-glazed Lustreware

These pieces present more obvious affinities with Islamic pottery. The forms are full-bellied and generous yet highly refined in their balance and proportions, with graceful handles, spouts and lips. The quality of the lustres pays tribute to Peascod's mastery of the technique but they are subtly and thoughtfully applied; they create another layer of visual tension which converses with the form.

My more traditional tin-glaze ceramics are made for lustre purposes. The same approach to bisque, re-glazing or re-firing is adopted until the surfaces are what I want. I use lead bisilicate frits in preference to calcium borate frits as they are notably more sensitive to the lustre reaction. I use very finely adjusted percentages or balances of tin versus zirconium silicate. High levels of tin (up to 10%) will produce grey to black surface colour in lustre reduction. When this is not required I prefer using 10% of zirconium silicate opacifier for a white background.

The lustre pots are always fired in woodfiring kilns especially designed for lustre purposes. A more recent innovation has been the use of forced draught for lustre firing. This has produced an inordinate control of the firing method as well as developing new lustre colours not normally seen in the softer natural draught lustre kilns. I use cypress or white pine for firing purposes.

I often feel tin is misunderstood or misused by many potters. I feel superior whites can be developed by using a zirconium opacifier. I use tin sparingly – usually as a colour reagent. Zirconium silicates are easier to use, fine and considerably cheaper.

I work constantly, test glaze permutations and surface finishes alongside the commitment to evolving my three-dimensional forms. In recent years I have begun to devote more time to hand finishing the work. I use many methods – most of which are largely intuitive. Quite often I don't even know what I'm doing as I have realised that too much thinking can inhibit or produce an over-contrived result.

Matthias Ostermann

Of German origin, Ostermann has been working in Canada since 1974. He trained and worked as a production potter for many years, using stoneware and porcelain, with strong leanings towards oriental forms and glazes. However, the narrative element, so much a characteristic of Ostermann's work, appeared early, as did a liking for the sgraffito technique. He always had a strong inclination to draw.

A study tour of Italy in 1981 was a turning point for Ostermann and opened his eyes to the bright colours of low-fired maiolica. He committed himself to this technique despite the long-standing prejudice against earthenware prevalent in North America at the time. The switch to maiolica also prompted the beginnings of a gradual change in his work from functional, where the decoration is servant to the form, to a perception of the ware as a pure vehicle for the rich painting. For a while, Ostermann's pots were as close to canvasses as he could make them so that he could experiment with freer painting, unhampered by the curves and protrusions of three-dimensional forms. Large, often oval, platters were painted with Italianate fruit – melons, bananas, plums, in a riot of colour.

Matthias Ostermann in his studio in Montreal.
Photograph by Jan Thijs.

From these he gradually began to build up a repertoire of three-dimensional surfaces for painting in the form of narrative vessels and sculptures. The development from the Mediterranean-style fruit to a more allegorical content reflects a personal rediscovery of a child-hood passion for myths, legends, fairy tales and dreams. (His mother had been a professional narrator in Germany and Ostermann as a child often acted as 'prompter' when she was rehearsing before recitals.) Stories from the Bible, European legends, Greek mythology, ethnic creation myths, even modern authors are reinterpreted through new imagery.

In adopting maiolica as a painting medium, Ostermann feels he is part of a long-standing tradition; the *istoriato* wares of Renaissance Italy were an important precedent for story-telling on pots. An affinity for German Expressionist painting and for the work of Chagall is also visible in Ostermann's style. He has also been influenced by the modern Italian painter, Paladino.

Although Ostermann, thriving on diversity, still produces both a thrown domestic range and architectural ceramics (tiles), the main focus for

Matthias Ostermann, 'Loup-Garou', ht 62cm, 1990.
Photograph by Paul Crouch.

Sketch for Loup-Garou.

Matthias Ostermann, detail of wall plate 'Centaur', diam. 45cm, 1990.
Photograph by Paul Crouch.

his work is on handbuilt structures. Recent totem-like, slab-built sculptures move completely away from the vessel and give more scope for imaginative and narrative elements in the painting. They have become a stimulus for even more intense colours and bolder painting.

Technical Notes

The pieces are most often slab-built or constructed from a combination of thrown and slab components. The shape, or 'canvas', usually two-sided, is loosely conceived to accommodate the intended painted image.

Ostermann's work does not have the conventional look of maiolica; the white background is only in evidence in the fine sgraffito lines, etched through the layers of colour for final definition. The palette is striking in its range and richness. Colours are built up and blended not only to cover the whole surface but to create a feeling of depth not dissimilar to that of an oil painting, but with the added qualities of light penetration and refraction inherent in maiolica. The tin glaze is used as a base to show off the

Matthias Ostermann, wall sculpture 'Angel and Serpent', ht 28cm, 1990.
Photograph by Paul Crouch

123

pigments to maximum brilliance; it also filters through and textures the pigments in interesting ways. Sometimes the already glaze-fired surface is repainted with thick, semi-transparent pigments and then refired for a more layered colour effect.

The colours are blended to a personal palette, using both oxides and commercial stains. Borax frit is added, more or less, according to the degree of surface gloss required. One to one is a standard melt. The density of the colour, ranging from translucent watercolour to thick oil-paint effects, depends on the amount of water used to dilute the pigment.

After applying the glaze, which is sometimes brushed on in stucco-fashion to further break up colour, an approximate design is sketched out in pencil. Basic colours are applied everywhere, using a soft brush. Darker colours (black, green) are then painted on as a kind of rough outline to bring the images into relief. Then, with a wet, clean brush (a household paintbrush or a Chinese brush), the colours are lightly blended into each other. They are sometimes also smudged with the fingers. Finally, the images are brought to life with a quickly etched sgraffito line, using a knitting needle or a bamboo knife.

The bisque firing is taken to a hot Cone 06 to expel the gases and thus help eliminate pinholing in the glaze.

Basic Maiolica Glaze (cone 06/04)

Borax frit	70
Flint	5
Ball clay	7.5
China clay	7.5
Zircopax or Zircosil 5	10

1–2% rutile is sometimes added to soften the whiteness.

Seger molecular formula:

KNaO	0.36	Al_2O_3	0.36	SiO_2	2.92
CaO	0.64	B_2O_3	0.63	ZrO_2	0.21

The clay is a white low-fire body which allows the glaze to be applied a bit more thinly, hence avoiding crawling and white-spot problems.

Matthias Ostermann, 'Mermaid' teapot, ht 38cm, 1991. Photograph by Jan Thijs.

Walter Ostrom

Sixteen years ago, the Canadian potter Walter Ostrom had his tin-glaze work rejected for a major exhibition because it was considered 'regressive'. Such was the prejudice against maiolica in North America at that time, where the Sino-Japanese aesthetic with its focus on form and subservience of surface to form still prevailed.

Ostrom's recent work is a lively example of decorative ceramics which makes use of illusionism and extended reference. 'The desire of the object to reach out and connect with many other kinds of things and situations . . . is characteristic of the decorative' (George Woodman, 'Ceramic Decoration and the Concept of Ceramics as a Decorative art'). In Ostrom's case, these connections embrace many sources within the field of ceramics and his concepts are expressed as new interpretations of historical genres. This strategy includes affectionate reworkings of pieces traditionally associated with tin glaze such as the *tulipière* or the flower brick, which in turn present information or comment about Tzu Chou pillow pots or vases.

In Ostrom's work, the spirit is playful and energetic, expressing a genuine personal enthusiasm for the rich diversity of ceramic history. Here, the theme of ceramic quotation – the 'pot on a pot' – is not so much didactic in content but more an expression of the maker's ambivalent stance. He is both participant and observer. Maiolica for Ostrom is ideally suited both to the exploration of these ideas and to the making of flower containers:

> . . . Earthenware is versatile; it works in the kitchen or the living room. Although both slipware and maiolica are traditional earthenware techniques, they differ widely in terms of process and historical association. For holding and garnishing the food we prepare and serve, I choose sturdily potted forms that emphasize material. The flower vases are made for the living room. Their potting is more refined and their form and decoration refer to aspects of the history of ceramics. Maiolica seems appropriate.

He describes his initial response to tin glaze:

> Nova Scotia is a province rich in earthenware clay. I began by making terra sigillata flowerpots and graduated to slip-decorated glazed serving pieces for the table. Although familiar with the other great earthenware tradition, maiolica, it was a meeting with Alan Caiger-Smith and seeing slides of Andrea Gill's work in the early 70's that put me over the edge. What appealed to me most was the no-apologies colour. Although I was using strongly coloured glazes, the colour seemed brighter, more intense on the white ground of maiolica. The effect seemed so joyful, energetic and positive.
>
> Maiolica was a new world, complex and rich with new materials, methods, traditions and aesthetics. It forced me to pay more attention to every aspect of my materials and firing, since, with low-fire, it is the chemistry and not just the fire that makes the melt. It also introduced me to decoration with its attendant notions of pattern, frame, field, space and ground and taught me the difference between shape and form.
>
> Pots from 15th and 16th century Spain and Italy showed me that, contrary to popular pottery opinion, great decoration has rescued many weak forms. They also challenged and undermined my belief in such popular 20th century design notions as 'less is more', 'form follows function' and 'truth to materials'. With regard to the latter, and considering that it originated as a material response to pure and precious porcelain, the triumph of maiolica demonstrates that you **can** 'make a silk purse out of a sow's ear'.

Ostrom is concerned about function as well as content:

> My pots are made to function in the everyday complex world of the home rather than in the one-dimensional world of the gallery or museum. A pot should never stop working. In use, it should contain, present and enhance both its contents and its context. A pot comes with all sorts of cultural information – social, economic, aesthetic. I try to keep in mind both the utilitarian and informational roles. . . .

The amount of resistance put up by museums, gallery owners and the media to actually showing a pot in use, is indicative of a culture where objects are validated by their visual role alone. I don't think that flowers in a vase are a prop; these days it is appropriate to be reminded that use-value is central to the tradition of craft.

Walter Ostrom, Fish Vase with Mediterranean Pot, ht 34cm, maiolica, 1990.
The yellow is a home-made lead antimony stain. The blue is a transparent royal blue glaze on top of the white glaze.
Photograph by Elaine Dacey Ostrom.

On Working Procedures

All pieces are constructed from thrown, altered and assembled parts. Because all his work is wheel-based, Ostrom enjoys analysing form in terms of thrown components. Once the form of the piece is completed, he tries a variety of techniques (terra sigillata, slips, glaze) to see what is best for that particular idea.

More and more I am finding that the glaze, body and firing range are not to be assumed. Some processes might be more appropriate to that idea than others. . . . If it is maiolica, everything is drawn out, applied to tiles and test fired. This allows for technical control. Then it goes on test work-pieces. These pieces I read to see what they say and make changes accordingly. There are two different considerations – the formal and the content. . . .Sometimes I change images to make a clearer statement while leaving the formal elements alone. The painting is as much a way of working out the idea as the constructing stage.

Technical Information

The clay needs to be very plastic to withstand the complex forming methods. As flower vases are the main focus for current work, the clay must be tight to prevent water seepage. (Unglazed bottoms are in addition coated with terra sigillata.)

Ostrom is lucky to have a local brick clay that is both very plastic and fires very tight. Other clays are added to raise the temperature and vary the particle size. It fires to a dark terracotta colour.

Clay body:

Lantz clay*	60–80
Cedar Heights Redart clay	10–20
Ball clay	0–20
China clay	0–10

* Local brick clay available from Shaw Brick, Engfield, Nova Scotia.
Bisque firing temperature: Orton cone 08

Glaze Recipe (fired to cone 05)

Ferro frit 3124	55
Ferro frit 3292	26
Whiting	7
Kaolin	12
Add:	
Zircopax/Superpax	13%
Rutile	0.25%

126

Seger molecular formula:

K_2O	0.03	Al_2O_3	0.342	SiO_2	2.35
Na_2O	0.23	B_2O_3	0.355		
Li_2O	0.01				
CaO	0.69				
MgO	0.01				
SrO	0.03				

The glaze is run through 40s, 60s and 80s mesh screens. As it tends to settle out, Epsom salts and/or Ben Aqua or Macaloid* are added to help suspension.

* Magnesium compound

Walter Ostrom, Flowerbrick, width 29cm, 1988.
'The flower bricks are classic Dutch shapes, often decorated with what I would like to think of as a tongue-in-cheek update of Chinoiserie, reflecting the fact that current taste favours folksy Tzu Chou as symbolic of Chinese ceramics rather than the eighteenth century Ch'ing models . . . As a variation I tried using my basket vases and stylized historical flowers, themselves emblematic of decorative traditions. It is not only appropriate to have pots of flowers decorating a vase, but especially appropriate when most people do not know what a flower brick is; then, the decoration becomes a diagram of function. . . .'
Photograph by Elaine Dacey Ostrom.

To facilitate glaze coverage, the pieces are dipped quickly but completely in water and left to stand for a few minutes. After pouring the inside, the piece is then dipped upside down to glaze the outside. This minimises the amount of glaze needed and eliminates the need to wax bottoms. The glaze is run through a 60s mesh screen prior to use.

After setting up, the piece is fettled and then thoroughly sprayed with CMC gum* solution (in a hand-held spritzer bottle). The piece is allowed to dry at least 24 hours before decorating. This provides a hard, dust-free surface for painting.

* CMC = Carboxymethylcellulose or SCMC = Sodium Carboxymethylcellulose, a glaze binder

Pigments

Mainly commercial stains mixed with frit 3124 or 3292 in Gill's recommended proportions: 40 stain, 60 frit.

Copper carbonate, and sulphates of copper, cobalt and manganese are also used. Ostrom also makes some of his own pigments, e.g. lead antimonate yellow.

In addition to the above pigments, coloured glazes, both clear and opaque are also used on top of the raw maiolica glaze. Pigments are used to outline and the glaze to fill in. The glazes give quite a different surface quality from that of the in-glaze pigments – more like liquid colour on top of the glaze.

CMC gum is added to the pigment solutions to prevent smearing and assist flow. Epsom salts prevent the colours from settling out. The following is a basic liquid Ostrom has ready for mixing the pigments to a paintable consistency:

1 part CMC solution*
1 part Ben Aqua or Macaloid solution**
2 parts water

* 4–5 tsp CMC gum powder to vortex of 1 litre water in a blender
** 8–9 tsp Macaloid or Ben Aqua to vortex as above to make thick solution.

Designs are sketched on to the sized surface with an 8B pencil. In order to minimize handling, painting is carried out with the piece either on a banding wheel or on its side in a basin lined with cotton quilting or similar soft material (as demonstrated in Piccolpasso's notebooks).

The glaze firing is rapid up to two cones below final temperature. Then Ostrom aims for a duration of at least one hour between each of the final cones.

Water soluble enamels are sometimes used in a third firing.

Walter Ostrom, tulipière, ht 23 cm, 1983.
'The tulipière is traditional Dutch maiolica. The decoration comprises unglazed clay spouts set against a classic vine motif, reminding us of the source of maiolica technology itself.'

Margrit Linck (1897–1980)

Unlike the majority of ceramicists who use tin glaze, Margrit Linck makes no use of the glaze surface to present a content. Neither does her work in any way make reference to the man-made world of ceramics or other artefacts. It is concerned first and foremost with primitive formal qualities, referring in a general way to the natural world of human and animal forms. Linck has been described as '. . . using clay as if there were no other material . . . as a parable for the process of creation. . . .'[1] When glaze is used, it is for the sole purpose of colluding symbiotically with the form.

Born in 1897 in the Canton of Berne, Linck's first contact with ceramics was with the local traditional Swiss slipware. As a child she used to watch potters at work in the Heimberg pottery, and it was here that she later returned to learn practical workshop skills. She studied at the Keramische Fachschule in Berne and went on to spend several years studying art and drawing in Munich and Berlin. Wherever she went she was drawn to looking at pots in museums. Her marriage to the sculptor Walter Linck in 1927 was a turning point for her ideas about ceramics and in 1935, after living in Paris for several years, she set up her own studio in Berne. This was considered rather extraordinary at the time, not only because she was a woman (and pottery had always been the domain of the male sex) but also because she now began to break so radically from tradition. The critical encouragement of her husband and, through him, contact with the international art scene, led to the development of a much more formal approach. Surrealism had its impact, as did the work of such artists as Giacometti, Braque and Miro (with whom she exhibited in 1949). She much admired the still-life paintings of Morandi. In common with many artists working at that time, she also acknowledges the tremendous influence of primitive art and in particular to the plastic arts of Africa and the South Seas.

The 1970s and 1980s saw the emergence of the tin-glazed Weisse Vasen and two fairly distinct styles – the very personal thrown and distorted vase forms, with their oblique, archaic (reductive) references to human forms, on the one

hand; and the production ware – vases, lamps, bowls – made with the help of assistants, on the other. These have an astonishing, almost industrial, precision about them – thrown, turned and assembled in often quite complex combinations, but with a truly Modernist concern for structure. They are still being made today to Linck's original designs.

Margrit Linck's use of tin-glazed earthenware is unusual in that the glaze, conventionally used as a backdrop for painted exploration, is valued

Margrit Linck in her workshop in Reichenbach, Berne, in conversation with her co-workers. Examples of the production ware can be seen on the bench.

solely for its ability to enhance form. Her work from the 1950s onwards was almost exclusively glazed with a plain white tin glaze – sometimes shiny but with solid opacity, sometimes matt and stone-like in surface quality.

'I like the colour white. Form for me is the most important thing; if the form is good, I can only use white, as coloured glazes would disturb me.' Concentrating as she did, on vase forms, she also felt that flowers were best displayed in white vases.

Historical precedents for this respectful treatment of tin glaze are not as uncommon as might at first be thought. Throughout the history of European tin glaze, in each country there have been whitewares which were either minimally decorated or left plain showing off the proportions of the form and the surface quality of the glaze to maximum advantage – for example, the *bianchi di Faenza* and the whitewares of Delft.

Note

[1] Walter Vogt, at the opening of Linck's exhibition at Galerie Kornfeld, Berne, 1979.

Margrit Linck, vase, ht 14.5cm, 1979.
Matt white tin glaze.

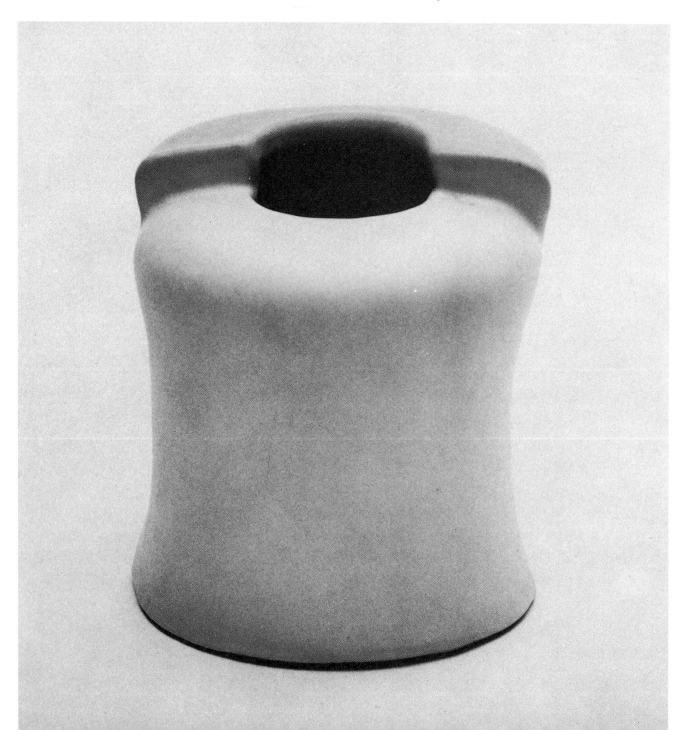

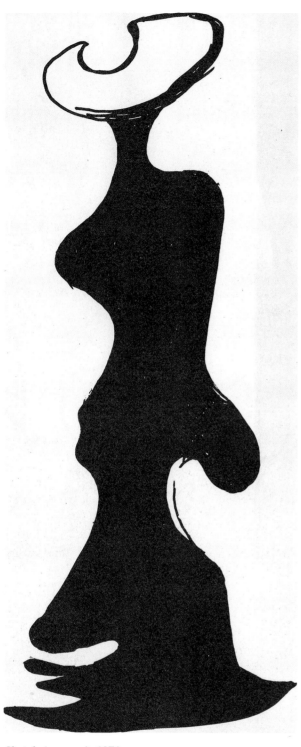

Sketch (woman), 1976.

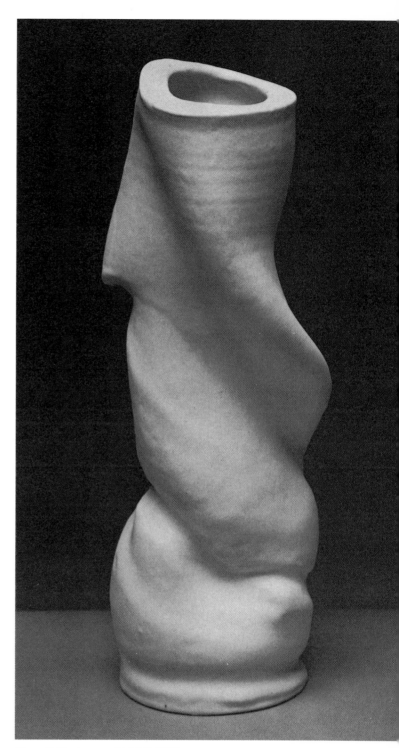

Margrit Linck, vase, ht 38.5, 1980.
Thrown and altered. Matt white tin glaze.

Photographs reproduced by kind permission of Frau Doktor Regula Linck.

Margrit Linck, vase, ht 37cm, 1964.
From the production range. Thrown and assembled.
Shiny white tin glaze. Linck saw this as a 'bridal' vase –
the bride's bouquet can be laid across the neck as well as
being arranged in the vase itself.

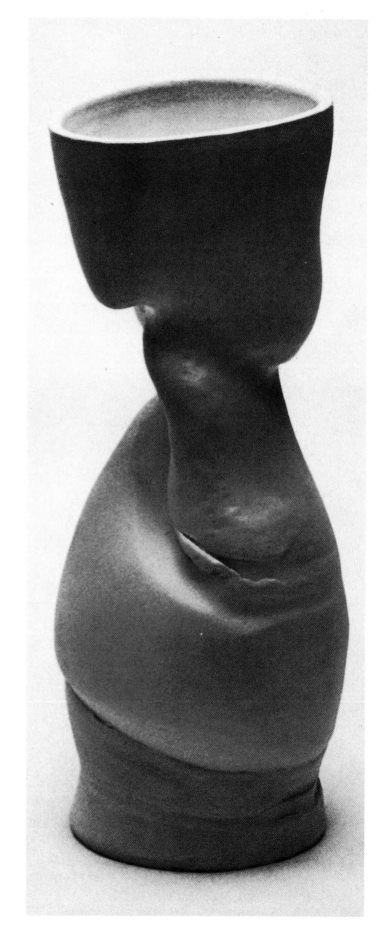

Margrit Linck, vase, ht 33cm, 1980.
Thrown and altered. Matt white tin glaze.

Daphne Carnegy

I came to maiolica via circuitous routes. My first conscious recognition of the medium, long before I started potting myself, was in the peasant pottery of Spain, Italy and France, whence it became forever associated in my mind with sun, sea and a certain element of hedonism. This imagined context is still significant, and acts as an instinctive driving force in my work.

A degree in French and several enjoyable years of pottery evening classes were my only qualifications when I got taken on as a trainee in the workshop of a 'faience' potter in the Mâconnais, France. The apprenticeship served in France gave me closer contact with both the tin-glaze and slipware traditions of Continental Europe and confirmed me in my desire to work in earthenware. On my return to England I attended the Harrow studio pottery course which gave me a broader perspective of ceramics and a good technical grounding; through a study of Italian maiolica, I also had the opportunity to carry out research into tin-glaze techniques and take a first few faltering steps in brushwork. Maiolica was a challenge on several levels: technically, contending with the many variable elements involved – bodies, glazes, pigments, firings; aesthetically, in the quest for some sort of personal and contemporary expression through brushwork (I was terrified of brushes); and ethically, braving it out in the face of considerable prejudice, maiolica at the time (1980) being frequently equated with homespun tweeness and amateurish efforts. It seemed to embody the very antithesis of Modernist principles, still prevalent and implicit in the Leach tradition, with its emphasis on formal rather than decorative qualities. When I started making, there was an apparent polarisation in ceramics – worthy utilitarian stoneware, glazed in celadons and tenmokus on the one hand, and Post-modernist abstract vessels of the Alison Britton/Elizabeth Fritsch variety. The *joie-de-vivre* of the post-Picasso revival had sunk into oblivion lacking a contemporary context. I wanted to combine the very decorative, exhilarating potential of maiolica with well-made pottery for everyday domestic use; its Mediter-

ranean palette would complement and enhance the good table.

Throwing for me is a highly enjoyable process. I gain as much satisfaction out of making a run of cups and saucers as I do out of throwing and decorating the more individual pieces. The forms are conceived of in terms of function but also as three-dimensional canvases and as such they are usually simple with little pre-imposed definition. This gives greater flexibility at the painting stage for either making use of the continuous surface or for creating a framework as desired. Recent pots have however taken on a more considered articulation of form – as for example in the flat-bottomed bowls and the beaked jugs, which are decorated in a more pre-determined way. I like strong, sturdy shapes, with a surface that still bears witness to the throwing process.

My decorative vocabulary of fruit, flowers and occasionally fish derives from their sensuous forms which can be simplified to suit my brush-work and used in either a fluid or a more formal manner. I find I am increasingly concerned with using elements or sections in a more abstract way, in terms of defined areas of colour which converse with the form. I appreciate the value of restraint as well as exuberance and I am more confident in leaving areas undecorated.

Underlying sources of reference, often coming from unconscious stores, are very eclectic but probably relate more to painting than to other arts – Cézanne, Matisse and Dutch still lifes of the 17th century. In the field of pottery, apart from an obvious affinity with Mediterranean peasant ware, I am drawn to archaic beginnings of traditions – early Islamic, Orvieto and Antwerp – when fresh, unself-conscious qualities are still dominant and before the inevitable onset of sophistication and refinement. On the other hand, the clean-cut precision of Staffordshire creamware and the extravaganzas of the Della Robbias also have a strong hold on my way of thinking.

Maiolica has a softness, depth and luminosity not to be found in other earthenware techniques. I am continually surprised at the variations of intensity and texture of the pigments as they fuse and shift with the glaze.

7

Daphne Carnegy, breakfast cups and saucers, 1991.
Photograph by Stephen Brayne, Courtesy Ceramic Review.

Opposite
Daphne Carnegy, dish, diameter 38 cm, 1992
Photograph by Stephen Brayne.

Technical Notes

I use a standard red earthenware body (Valentines) which is bisqued to 970°C. After the bisque firing, bottoms and feet are first rubbed down with wet and dry paper and then waxed with a mixture of hot wax and paraffin. The generous waisted feet of bowls and plates are so designed as to enable a good supporting grip when glazing, which is carried out with tongs.

The main glaze I use, which is a modification of a Caiger-Smith recipe, has a good colour response and a very wide firing range: from 1060°C to 1140°C: I fire to cone 01.

Lead bisilicate	60
Standard borax frit	9
Cornish stone	15
China clay	5
Tin oxide	7
Zirconium silicate	7
Zinc oxide	2
Bentonite	2

Seger molecular formula:

PbO	0.68	Al_2O_3	0.24	SiO_2	2.55
KNaO	0.11	B_2O_3	0.08	ZrO_2	0.15
CaO	0.11			SnO_2	0.18
ZnO	0.10				

Satin cream version

As above but replace the tin and zirconium silicate with tin oxide 4%, zirconium silicate 3% and titanium dioxide 3%. This is similar to the glaze A used for the colour tests on page 85.

Another glaze formulated for use on tiles: (1060°C–1080°C)

Lead bisilicate	75
Cornish stone	10
China clay	5
Tin oxide	10

Seger molecular formula:

PbO	0.94	Al_2O_3	0.23	SiO_2	2.44
KNaO	0.04			SnO_2	0.29
CaO	0.02				

For painting, I use both oxides and commercial stains. The oxides alone give a somewhat limited palette and the unadulterated commercial colours can be very crude, so they complement each other. I also intermix the two, varying proportions according to mood, thus retaining some element of unpredictability. Detailed information regarding pigments, painting and other techniques is given in Section II.

Bruce Cochrane

Cochrane's pieces look as if they were made for the banqueting table. They are functional but have a rare elegance and refinement. Undulating ovoid lidded dishes are elevated to the ranks of show-pieces, standing proudly on tall pierced feet. Handles, rims and lips take on extra ornamental significance, often loosely symbolising the intended contents of the vessel. Precedence for such florid functionalism in the service of high culinary art goes back to European faience and porcelain tableware of the 18th and 19th centuries. Cochrane's containers, like their ancestors, are not only meticulously thought out with precise food functions in mind – butter dishes, terrines, soup tureens etc. – but are designed in the spirit of formal grandeur and exotic ornament. Truly decorative pottery. 'To be decorative is to play a role. A decorative pot enters a room under certain rules that allow its admission. It performs a function there. It is something like the guest you might invite to your salon because he or she will play a specific role in the evening's soiree. . . .' (George Woodman, op. cit.)

Daphne Carnegy, beaked jug, ht 25 cm, 1992.
Photograph by Stephen Brayne.

Bruce Cochrane, soup tureen on stand,
36cm x 18cm, ht 31cm, 1989.
Maiolica and terra sigillata.
Photograph by Peter Hogan.

In spite of the complexity of their construction, which entails shaping, cutting and reassembling, Cochrane's pieces retain the vigour and immediacy of the throwing process (and in this respect, they have a kinship with Walter Keeler's work).

I do very little designing outside the studio. During the slow process of producing a pot, I have the chance to discover possibilities for other pieces with entirely different functions. As a result, I find myself being more inventive with form, relying less on historical examples; however those references are still important. (*Ceramics Monthly*, November 1990)

In contrast to the ceramics of, say, Gill and Ostrom, the tin glaze here is exploited, not for its value as an outer skin inviting further exploration with painting, but for its inherent quality as a form enhancer. Cochrane also works with terra sigillata, and the two surface treatments are used as alternative and contrasting ways of 'dressing' the same form. On the tin-glazed pieces, the use of unglazed, terra sigillata-coated areas (notably handles, lips, feet, sprigs) conveys the plasticity of the clay and emphasises detail in the form, which would otherwise have been considerably softened by an overall use of tin glaze. When Cochrane does indulge in inglaze decoration, it is in the form of simple, overlapping patterns sponged with cobalt and copper solutions to create a rich-textured surface, the copper sinking down into the glaze and the cobalt floating on the surface.

Bruce Cochrane, elevated entrée dish, 31cm x 12.5cm, ht 25.5cm, 1989. Maiolica and terra sigillata. Photograph by Peter Hogan.

Technical Information

Earthenware body (Cone 06–04)

Ball clay	10
Cedar Heights Redart clay	70
Plainsman Redstone clay	20

Add:

Ferro frit 3124	3
(for fired strength and density)	
Talc	5
Red iron oxide	0.25
(for richer colour)	

Matthias's Maiolica Glaze (Cone 05)

Ferro Frit 3124	74
Ball clay	7.5%
Edgar Plastic Kaolin (EPK)	7.5%
(China clay)	
Zircopax or Zircosil 5	.11

Add: Rutile (to soften white)	0.5%

Seger molecular formula:
(approximate)

KNaO	0.36	Al_2O_3	0.34	SiO_2	2.55
CaO	0.64	B_2O_3	0.63	TiO_2	0.04
				ZrO_2	0.20

Bruce Cochrane, salad bowl,
36cm x 18cm, ht 20.5cm, 1990.
Maiolica and terra sigillata.
Photograph by Peter Hogan.

Bruce Cochrane, butter/pate dish,
118cm, 1990.
Maiolica and terra sigillata.
Photograph by Peter Hogan.

138

Agalis Manessi

There is a gentle domesticity to Agalis Manessi's pots. Coiled and pinched into simple, soft shapes, they could represent primitive archetypes of the jug, the dish, the vase. Even after glazing the marks of the making process are visible and form a rhythmic, textured background to the painted imagery. For Manessi, the glazed pots are like primed canvasses waiting to receive images to be looked into, in the case of bowls, or around, in the case of vases and jugs. She distances herself from the objects in a playful (but serious – not flippant) way; pots are painted with familiar still-life images of other pots, bowls of fruit, shells and feathers, only to become part of a larger still-life when placed in their domestic setting. Each artefact has its own character and speaks of itself but it also has an extended role in both suggesting its environment and functioning on a decorative level in the specific context of the living room or kitchen. The process can be seen as a self-conscious creation of the decorative pot. Some pieces are less ironic and carry portraits of people, both observed and imagined, which stare out with Byzantine directness or look sideways, inviting inquiry as to what lies around the curve. The shape of the well of a dish will often suggest images to Manessi – for example, vases or heads – which fill that space and which in turn suggest ways of completing the 'picture'.

The style of the painting is delicate yet factual, the palette restrained and subtle, with its dirty yellows, greys and flesh tones – a far cry from the primary colours of the Italianate schools. The association is more with the gentler palette of English delftware.

Manessi used to work in sgraffito slipware, which to her was very clear-cut and predictable in terms of finished appearance. She was attracted to the freshness of maiolica which, 'like ballet, looks effortless and disguises the complexity of the technique'.

Agalis Manessi, dish, shell and feathers, 1991.

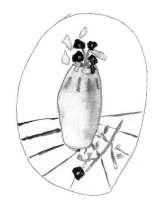

Agalis Manessi.
From the sketchbook

Technical Notes

Red earthenware body, bisque fired to 1000°C.

The glaze is a commercial one – Potterycrafts P2023 tin glaze, fired to 1060°C with ½ hour soak. A wide range of oxides, underglaze colours and body stains are used, usually diluted with a little glaze and water. Potassium dichromate (NB poisonous) gives the rather murky yellow.

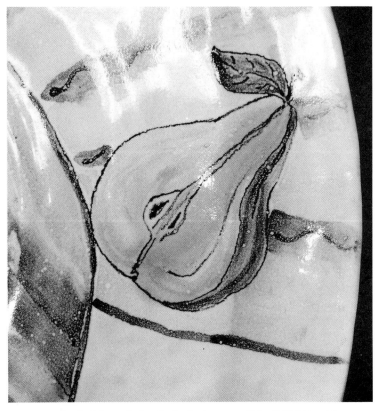

Agalis Manessi, detail of painting on a dish, 'Still Life with Vase and Pear Half', 1987.

Morgen Hall

Morgen Hall makes quirky, whimsical pots which aspire to the magnificent. They are expressive of their maker's technical virtuosity and meticulous attention to detail, yet without a trace of pedantry. Hall's overriding concerns are with complexities of form and extravagant, sometimes burlesque ornament; surface treatment is employed in their service and is far removed from the traditional appearance of maiolica. Here, the function of the tin glaze, rather like that of a salt glaze, is in part to give emphasis to surface textures and variations of relief in the form. The use of slips under the glaze reinforces the integration of surface with form and at the same time provides a depth of relief which is both tempered and enhanced by the tin glaze. The creamy white glaze allows the richness of the red earthenware body to filter through where the glaze breaks on edges or is applied thinly. Stark colour contrasts are softened both by the glaze and further by the application of yellowy-orange pigments on top of the glaze. The general effect is not dissimilar to the surface quality and tones of a high-fired Shino-type glaze.

A love of pattern is evident, and the patterns work hand in hand with the intricacies of the form. Some are bold and make statements in themselves – like the spirals and serpentine shapes. Some work with whole sections of the pot as if they were overall textile designs. All are abstract, anonymous even, in the way that some very simple peasant pottery motifs are.

In spite of the complexity of their construction, Hall's pots are all eminently functional and are intended for everyday use.

Technical Notes

With the exception of some press-moulded non-circular pieces, all the work is thrown and turned. A blue slip is applied to the raw pots using resist (paper, polythene, latex or Copydex), brush, slip trailing or sgraffito methods. After the bisque firing (cone 06), the glaze is applied before the final addition of sponged or brushed glaze stains. These are commercial stains (yellows and oranges) mixed with a little rutile and some of the base glaze. The addition of lithium carbonate to the glaze helps to bring out the orange tones of the clay through the glaze.

Blue slip

Valentine's red earthenware	60	
Ball clay	40	
Cobalt oxide	7%	approximately
Manganese dioxide	4%	

(Each batch of slip is tested and colours are adjusted if necessary. Red iron oxide is added if the blue is too bright.)

Morgen Hall, teapot, teacup and saucer, 1991.
Photograph by Peter Russell.

Glaze recipe (fired to cone 01)

(based on a recipe by Alan Caiger-Smith)

Lead bisilicate	56
Flint	8
Cornish stone	10
Standard borax frit	8
Zinc oxide	4
Tin oxide	8
Lithium carbonate	5

Seger molecular formula:

PbO	0.50	Al_2O_3	0.10	SiO_2	1.90
K_2O	0.02	B_2O_3	0.06	SnO_2	0.16
Na_2O	0.05				
Li_2O	0.21				
CaO	0.07				
ZnO	0.15				

Morgen Hall, lidded jar, ht 50 cm, 1991.
Photograph by Peter Russell.

Gallery

Jitka Palmer

Jitka Palmer is not concerned with perfection. Her work is first and foremost about drawing in a free and lively manner. As a painting medium, maiolica gives her the most scope for colour and texture. Having felt restricted by small thrown pieces, she is currently making very large oddly-shaped coiled platters and dishes whose expanse, asymmetry and looseness are more in sympathy with the intention of the painting; the flattish surface more akin to the canvas. Palmer has intentionally relaxed her shapes in order to keep up with the pace of her drawings.

The drawings all have a human element and are an imaginative recreation from all sorts of personal experiences – poetry, music, fiction, real-life observation, dreams. Recurrent themes are the family, devils, birds – a personal folklore of Chagallian mode. Picasso's ceramics have also been influential as have several Czech painters. There is no attempt in Palmer's painting to create a picture plane or the illusion of perspective. The imagery is free-floating, adapting itself to the irregular contours of the piece itself.

Technical Notes

The colours are applied and built up in a painterly manner not dissimilar to the technique of oil painting. The tin glaze is brushed on very thickly in places. In contrast, some areas are just covered with a trasparent glaze to reveal the pleasing orange colour of the body. Then more glazes – low-firing coloured glazes from Czechoslovakia (notably a crimson and a green) are brushed on top of the tin glaze. These give a very different surface quality from the pigment mixtures which are also painted on at this stage – antimony yellow, cobalt blue, grey-green, and a murky yellow (a mixture of antimony yellow, crimson and iron). Mop brushes are used for large areas of colour; soft banding brushes for outlines. Finally, lines are sgraffitoed through the pigments to give extra definition.

Clay body

For the large platters, a high-firing red earthenware body (Potterycrafts) is mixed with one-third grogged white earthenware (Potclays) or Y material (Potclays).

Bisque firing:	1050–1080°C

Glaze

The glaze is based on a traditional Czech formula:

PbO	0.80	Al_2O_3	0.33	SiO_2	2.36
K_2O	0.03	B_2O_3	0.17	SnO_2	0.28
Na_2O	0.05				
CaO	0.13				

Recipe:

Lead bisilicate	65.00
High alkaline frit	3.8
Calcium borate frit	5.4
China clay	15.00
Tin oxide	10.00
Flint	2.5
Glaze firing:	970–990°C

Jitka Palmer, 'From Life', diam. 36 cm, 1991.

Stanley Mace Andersen

Pattern and colour are fundamental to Stanley Mace Andersen's pottery. The forms are well-made, sturdy updated versions of country pottery; the painting is vibrant, urban – light-hearted but considered. Initially attracted to high-fire porcelain, he was first introduced to maiolica through the work of Andrea Gill. He found that the move to low-fire and maiolica entailed more than a mere technical change:

> There was something about the medium that lightened my hand. From the start my decorations on earthenware were less serious, less somber than anything I had done on porcelain. (*Studio Potter*, vol. 11, no.2, 1983)

Andersen is primarily concerned with making utilitarian ware for the table and kitchen, although he makes a distinction between his regular lines and certain 'limited edition' pieces, such as the coffee pots, which are more challenging and stimulating to make. Throwing retains a flexibility of form which can evolve in response to the changing aesthetic ideas of the maker. He mixes his own red earthenware body, biscuit fires to cone 04 and glaze fires to cone 03. The glaze is leadless and zirconium-opacified.

Stanley Mace Andersen, coffee pot and demi-tasses, 1992. Photograph by Bart Kasten. (See other photograph on p. 146.)

I use this technique and fire to this temperature because it provides me not only with a range of bright, sharp colors to use in developing the patterns and designs I paint on my pots, but also because it allows me more freedom and control over my treatment of the surfaces. I try to achieve a balance between simple forms and their decorated surfaces and to convey a casual, playful quality.

After fourteen years of making domestic ware and working in maiolica, Andersen still continues to find new directions within the medium.

Glaze recipe

Ferro frit 3124	55
Ball clay	10
Flint	10
Zircopax	8
(Zircosil 5	1)

Seger molecular formula:
(approximate)

KNaO	0.37	Al_2O_3	0.29	SiO_2	3.38
CaO	0.63	B_2O_3	0.62	ZrO_2	0.21

Terry Siebert

I am a potter who likes to paint, so it was quite natural for me to begin working with maiolica glazes. The white glaze serves as a canvas for colorful painting. The fired glaze is characterized by brilliant, watery colors and a lush surface which has a depth and richness uncommon to most low-fire glazes.

The history of maiolica-glazed earthenware is as captivating as the glaze itself. Many of the forms and patterns I use have their roots in ancient Persian, Spanish and Italian ceramics and decorative arts traditions. My pottery forms echo the strong, simple shapes of European folk pottery. I like full-bodied forms with prominent bases, rims and spouts and thick, gestural handles. The patterns and motifs I use to decorate these forms are a synthesis of my own observations of nature and historical influences. I strive for decoration that interacts with the pottery form and enlivens its surface. To try and create an illusion of depth, I layer pattern upon pattern and employ *trompe l'oeil* painting techniques.

Many of my designs are inspired by the garden: a realm where man and nature unite to create an idealized vision of nature. Harlequin and checkerboard patterns provide a counterpoint for the floral and plant motifs and refer to the architectural elements of a garden (tilework, pavement, trellises etc).

The tulip is a favorite flower which I find to be both cheerfully simple and extravagantly exotic. It has a powerful, gestural form that is easily translated into decorative motifs, embellishing everything from 17th century Dutch paintings to 20th century toilet paper. The tulips I paint evolve from my knowledge of history and a lot of time observing and painting real tulips. I remain intrigued by this sentimental and sublime flower.

Technical Notes

Terracotta clay body (cone 06–03)

Cedar Heights Redart clay	64
Old Mine 4 ball clay	14
AP Green fireclay	9
Talc	9
Spodumene	4
plus (optional)	
Barium carbonate	0.5
Muddox 28-mesh grog	5

Glaze (cone 06–03)

Ferro frit 3124	72
Flint	10
Edgar (EPK) Plastic Kaolin (China clay)	12
Zircopax or Zircosil 5	10

Seger molecular formula:
(approximate)

K_2O 0.36	Al_2O_3 0.35	SiO_2 3.06
CaO 0.64	B_2O_3 0.63	ZrO_2 0.21

Black glaze

As above, but substitute 8% Mason black stain #6650 for the Zircopax.

Firing temperatures: Biscuit cone $05\frac{1}{2}$, glaze cone 04. Optional sintering firing to 018. This hardens the glaze sufficiently to make the painting easier.

Siebert currently uses oxides of vanadium, copper, chrome and cobalt in addition to a range of stains. Stains are mixed with frit 3124 in 25/75 ratio. Add water as required plus a tablespoon of laundry starch for every 100 g.

Terry Siebert, 'Parterre/Harlequin' vase, ht 70 cm, 1988. Photograph by Roger Schreiber.

Terry Siebert,
'Tulips and Lattice' bowl,
diam 31 cm, 1992.
Photograph by Roger Schreiber.

Stanley Mace Andersen,
serving bowl, diam 31 cm, 1992.

Majolica Works

left

Majolica Works, large platter, diam. 46 cm.
Liam Curtin and Wendy Jones produce a wide range of domestic ware as well as tiles, murals and mosaics. Most pots are thrown; large dishes are press-moulded and standard tableware items such as plates and bowls are jolleyed. They use a standard red earthenware with a lead-based tin glaze fired to 1140°C. Both oxides and commercial stains are used for painting.

Gail Barwick

below

Gail Barwick (Australia), platter 40 cm by 50 cm, 1991.
Barwick's admiration for old meat dishes and her fascination with oriental rugs, mosaics and textiles, led her to work in the format of large platters, which she treats as open canvases for experiments in colour and pattern. The clay is a mixture of terracotta and stoneware. Glaze firing is to 1100–1120°C.

Recipe

Ferro Frit 4712	90
China clay	10
Tin oxide	5%

Powdered stains are mixed with frit and glycerine.

Richard and Carol Selfridge

(see photograph on p. 151)

After working in traditional domestic stoneware and porcelain for 12 years, Richard and Carol Selfridge's interest in painting and drawing and their search for additional colour possibilities led them to maiolica. In it they have found the perfect medium for the gentle humour of their large, constructed pieces. These are all about illusion, form and altered perception. Content takes its cue from the silhouette of the pot – a roundness will suggest a woman's flank or a zebra's arching neck; a handle becomes a snake, horn or hair – and is interwoven with secret references and symbols relating to the makers' own lives.

The tall, segmented pots are constructed from ready-made components of flying saucers (made from joining two press-moulded dishes), which are cut and altered to create gesture and articulation.

> We like the way they look much like a pot in a painting by Matisse, Braque or Picasso. With their cut-down front rim and their slightly comical handles, they become a kind-spirited caricature of historic 'real' pots. Our pots usually have an illusionistic 'pot-on-a-pot' front side and the reverse side often becomes a shaped canvas for figurative/narrative painting. We are definitely interested in painting flat things to look round and round things to look flat. Through color, pattern, shading, figure and ground, the viewer is given clues as to the nature and dimensions of things, a picture which she will complete with her own constructed reality.

Technical Notes

The Selfridges use a local brick clay from Athabasca, Alberta, to which they add $\frac{1}{2}\%$ barium carbonate (anti-scumming), 5% ferro frit 3124 (to tighten the body) and 15% fine grog (for tolerance). For the large pieces, nylon fibre is added for tensile strength to counteract the stress of drying.

Bisque firing is to cone 08.

Glaze recipe: (cone 04)

Barium carbonate	3
Tile #6 Kaolin	19
(China clay)	
Ferro Frit 3134	11
Ferro Frit 3124	62
Flint	5
Superpax or Zircosil 5	16

Add rutile $\frac{1}{4}\%$ to soften the whiteness.

Bentonite, laundry starch or sizing is added to harden the painting surface.

Stains are made from the base glaze (without the opacifier) plus 5–15% glaze stains (Masons) or oxides. Glycerine is added for flow.

Paul Rozman

Coffee pot by Canadian potter, Paul Rozman, 1986.
The tin glaze is rich enough to clothe and enhance the form without further statement.

Deirdre Daw

In her work, Daw acknowledges a variety of influences including 'Islamic art, Hispano-Moresque pottery and architecture, topiary, Antonio Gaudi, non-art events in life and dreams'. Of maiolica she says: 'Maiolica has fresh color, strong vivid clear marks – showing every tremor of your hand. The way it can be worked to develop a sense of depth with the red earthenware clay underneath, the white glaze and then all the different layers of color is beyond anything possible with PAINT!'

Shapes are thrown and/or handbuilt. Biscuit firing is to cone 07; glaze firing to cone 04.

Daw developed her own clay body for a good glaze fit.

Clay body: (06–03)

Cedar Heights Redart	65
Hawthorne (fireclay)	10
Old mine #4 (ball clay)	15
Talc	5
Nepheline syenite	5
plus Bentonite	2%

Glaze (Andrea Gill's with minor alterations): Cone 04

Ferro Frit 3124	65.75
Kona F4 Felspar (Soda Felspar)	17.14
Edgar Plastic Kaolin (EPK) (China clay)	10.82
Nepheline syenite	6.29
Add tin oxide (or Superpax 7%, Tin 7%)	10%
Golden brown stain	¼–½%
V-Gum-T	½–¼%

(UK: this material, a magnesium alumina silicate, is unavailable in the UK – use 2% bentonite instead)

Stains and oxides are mixed with 60% frit (3124 or 3110) and a bit of CMC gum solution. Daw also makes use of terra sigillata, low-fire glazes and enamels. The glaze is sprayed, dipped or painted on, depending on the desired effect.

Deirdre Daw (USA), untitled, ht 16.5 and 20.5 cm, 1991. Reversible double-walled carved saucers. Photograph courtesy of Jacques Gael Cressaty.

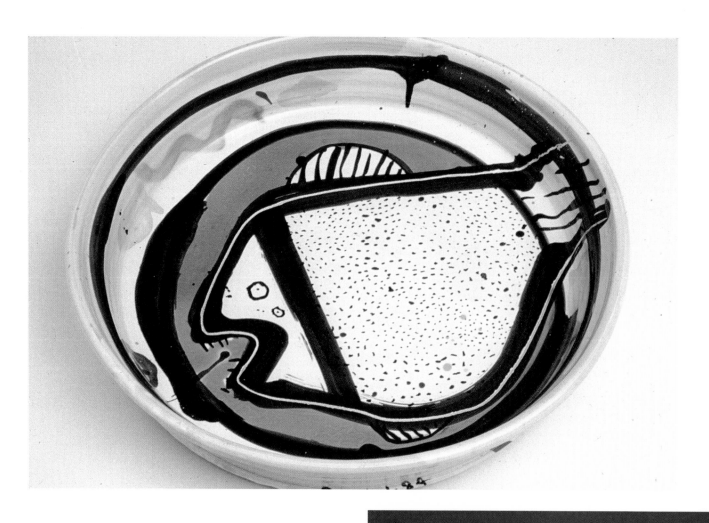

Jason Shackleton

Jason Shackleton trained at Dartington (now Dart) Pottery and went on to work first with Mary Wondrausch and then with Alan Caiger-Smith at Aldermaston before setting up his own pottery in Dumfries, Scotland. He works in both slipware and tin glaze making domestic ware and one-off pieces which often incorporate handbuilding techniques as well as throwing. He also makes tiles and murals. In common with Caiger-Smith, Shackleton wood fires his tin-glazed earthenware. He uses Fremington clay, biscuit-fired to 960°C and a lead/tin glaze, fired to 1080°C. Painting pigments are all colouring oxides ground on tiles with water and a little gum arabic solution (see p. 93).

Jason Shackleton, Waterfall pot, ht 23 cm, 1988.

Right
Carol and Richard Selfridge, Circus Performers Desertion,
ht 79 cm, 1990.

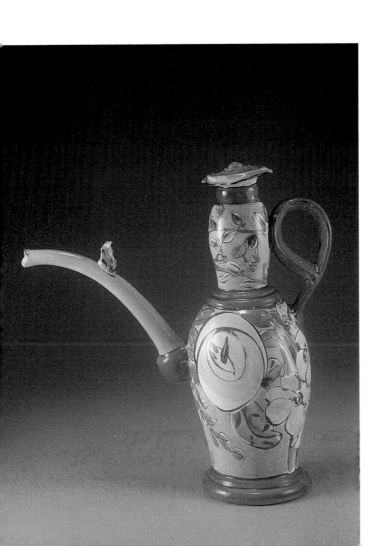

Linda Arbuckle

'Ideas about the value of indulgence in humanizing daily
life, and enjoyment of line and color are important
considerations to me. While my forms tend to be
controlled, the surface tells the form not to take itself so
seriously, and loosens up with color, calligraphic line,
image and composition to make the piece dance. Life is a
balancing act between discipline, expression and
entertaining one's self within these pursuits.'

Linda Arbuckle (USA) 'More Feminine', ht 33 cm, 1992.

151

Hylton Nel

Hylton Nel (South Africa), plates, diam 18 cm, 1992.
Press-moulded. Blue in-glaze painting on tin glaze.
By kind permission of the photographer David Cripps and Contemporary Applied Arts, London.

Ian Symons

Canadian potter Ian Symons is interested in colour, pattern and painting, and the maiolica work represents only a part of his range of pottery.

'I admire and study historical tureens, in particular 18th century French faience tureens, such as those made in eastern France at Niderviller. With my tureens I try to create a presence that refers to the Rococo flamboyance of the historic examples yet has a humble folk pottery element to it also. I make these pots to be used regularly so I do not want the pieces to be intimidating to handle; I want them to be inviting, and to be touched. One of maiolica's subtle qualities is that it is tactile painting. It is important to me that the pot maker and the ceramic painter are the same person – there is a dialogue between the painter and the potter which encourages the forms to improve so they become better objects for painting; the

painter becomes more aware of the three-dimensional qualities of the pot. For example, earlier tureens portrayed decorative panels as rigid reiterations of the form; now the "panels" whilst still containing the spirit of the form now have a sense of movement and dynamism.'

Pattern and image ideas are sketched out on paper. Then Symons warms up to painting by drawing on paper with maiolica colours, using the same brushes that he will use on the pot. He begins painting on the pot with a wash of food colouring to block out areas and indicate a general layout, before switching to the ceramic colours.

Ian Symons, tureen, ht 26 cm, l 39 cm, w 17 cm, 1989. Press-moulded red earthenware. Maiolica painting on zirconium base glaze, fired to 1050°C.

153

Reptile (Carlo Briscoe and Edward Dunn)

The tiles are made from a grogged white stoneware body – rolled out and cut with a stencil. The format of the design is similar to early Dutch examples, but Briscoe has created a whimsical, contemporary style in her miniature pictures. Both oxides and underglaze colours have been used.

A Reptile glaze recipe: (1020°C)

Lead bisilicate	88
China clay	5
Tin oxide	7

Seger formula:

| PbO | 1 | Al_2O_3 | 0.16 | SiO_2 | 2.01 |
| | | | | SnO_2 | 0.18 |

Pigments:
Naples yellow:

Antimony oxide	5.5g
Lead oxide	10g
Tin oxide	3g

Black:

| Manganese dioxide | 6 |
| Cobalt oxide | 1 |

Reptile (Carlo Briscoe and Edward Dunn), diamond picture tiles, painted by Carlo Briscoe, 1991.

Pippin Drysdale

From a fine-art background, Drysdale lives and works in Fremantle, Western Australia. Her expressive work is inspired by direct experiences and by the environment. In 1991, Drysdale travelled extensively in order to expand her creative horizons. After working in Italy, she went on to lecture and exhibit in Russia. The flamboyance of both the Italian and Russian cultures have been a significant factor in her recent work.

Pippin Drysdale, bowl, Effigy series 92, diam. 49 cm, ht 14 cm, black and white tin glaze with lustres, 1992.
Western Australian Art Gallery and Museum collection.

Gilbert Portanier

In 1948, after studying fine art and architecture at the Beaux Arts de Paris, Portanier set up his studio in Vallauris. His encounters with Picasso were a decisive influence on the course of his ceramics, which make use of many forms of expression, combining techniques of – sculpture, pottery and painting. Pieces are often produced as part of an on-going exploration of a current theme – for example, music, fashion, the theatre, masks, and as such have a narrative/figurative content which refers outside the world of ceramics.

On the medium of maiolica he is lyrical:

> 'J'excerce la faïence stannifère parcequ'elle se prête aux exercices périlleux et combinatoires, aux mutations analogues, aux douceurs satinées d'un pinceau migrateur à la surface poudrée de l'email; la cuisson révèle par osmose les couleurs minerales diluées sur sa blancheur diaphane.'

Technical notes:

The body is a dolomitic earthenware, red or white. The glaze is opacified with tin or zircon. Bisque and glost temperatures are 1030°C, in an electric kiln. Natural colouring oxides are used in the painting (along with *beaucoup de temps et de passion*).

Right
Gilbert Portanier, Masque, ht 40 cm, 1989.

Below
Gilbert Portanier, Balançoire, ht 40 cm, 1989.

Jane Gustin

Gustin approaches ceramics from a painterly point of
view, exploiting the layered depth and richness of
maiolica colour to convey concepts of motion and time.
The pigments are adjusted and overlapped to create an
impression of wet paint. An increasing interest in the
modulation of form by colour is leading Gustin to work
with more awareness of three-dimensional surfaces.
Gustin also makes vases, tiles and tableware.

Jane Gustin, platter, diam. 60 cm, hump-moulded.

Jane Gustin (USA), platter, diam. 60 cm, hump-moulded.

158

Tradition and Innovation
Some Aspects of Workshop and Factory Production

So far, the contemporary tin-glaze work discussed has been within certain parameters which can roughly be defined as studio pottery – work which, even though it may be produced in multiplicity, is essentially the expression of an individual and craft-based vision. I was curious to find out what was happening in the realm of the more pluralistic, anonymous type of production: on the one hand, the small family workshop working in a vernacular idiom; and on the other, the much larger-scale manufactories who have a considerable weight of high-art tradition behind them. Does peasant pottery still exist? Historicism abounds – what is the value of reproducing historical models? Is the overwhelmingly strong tradition of tin-glazed earthenware being reassessed or confronted in any way in the light of contemporary design for production? Without intending in any way to be comprehensive or creating wider inference, I have chosen to look at some isolated examples of these more popularist areas of tin-glaze production – vernacular pottery of Spain and Italy; current production at the Grazia factory in Deruta, Italy; and innovative design projects at Nevers and Quimper through the work of artist Marc Camille Chaimowicz.

Vernacular Potteries
in Spain and Italy

In every country that has had a strong tradition of tin-glazed earthenware there has been a marked cycle of evolution and devolution. Initial imitation and adaptation of Italianate sources combined with national characteristics to create a high-status art form which then went on to enjoy a 'golden age'. Changing tastes and demands ushered in a decline of artistic standards and loss of prestige. Although there was no longer a fashion demand from the middle and upper classes, the needs of ordinary people for useful pottery still existed. Tin-glazed pottery was still produced but now within the framework of a vernacular idiom where it became fused with popular culture. In most countries this tradition persisted throughout the 19th century and well into the 20th. The essence

Flat-bottomed dish with rolled-over rim, diam 30 cm. Spanish (Triana) late 19th century.
Freely painted in blue, green, yellow and dark brown. The clay is pale, rough and sandy, the tin glaze not very dense.
Photograph by Douglas Cape.

of this peasant pottery lay in the intuitive, fluent decoration and the simple functionality of the shapes, tried and tested throughout the generations. Its unpretentiousness and crude vigour are qualities for which many contemporary potters have a certain nostalgia. Some base their work firmly in this tradition and make direct reference to the 'peasant' aesthetic in their work. Today the grass-roots function of peasant pottery is obsolete; as it no longer fulfils a genuine need, and in order to ensure survival, it turns increasingly to the lucrative tourist industry and to the reproduction of historical designs.

Spain and Italy have always had a strong peasant pottery tradition based on family structures – knowledge and skills were handed down from one generation to the next; tradition was preserved due to virtual immunity to external influences; supply was in accordance with local demand. Today, only a relatively small number of family-run workshops survive; the Spanish potter Artigas [1] writing in 1970 tells us that in Triana, a famous tin-glaze centre since the 16th century which right up until the 1960s boasted as many as 30 fabricas, he could only locate three still in existence. This seems to be a fairly typical example of the situation throughout Spain. Villages are no longer isolated. The consumer market has changed; there is no longer any real need for utilitarian pots (apart from some unglazed wares such as the eminently functional water bottles), and the shift has been to the tourist trade with a consequent compromising of aesthetic integrity, particularly in the case of maiolica. In many cases, production has been turned over to reproduction of old designs, as in Talavera and Paterna, Triana and Manises. However, some examples of the original simplicity, vigour and instinctive calligraphic qualities of the peasant tradition can still be found, and, thanks to Artigas and numerous articles about Spanish potteries, there has been renewed interest (and custom) from an informed public. Italian potteries were on the whole much quicker to capitalise on the tourist potential and market a more refined and streamlined product, although in so doing losing much of the casual simplicity of the old country pottery.

Bowl, diam. 20cm, Guadix, 1970s.
Painted in cobalt on a thin tin glaze, pinky body showing through.

Serving dish, diam. 40 cm. Massa Lubrense (Italy) 1960s.
Simplistic fruit designs in vivid colours characterise the Massa Lubrense ware which is still produced today.
Photograph by Douglas Cape. Private collection.

160

MAIOLICHE ARTISTICHE ARTIGIANALE – THE GRAZIA FACTORY, DERUTA

Deruta was one of the most important centres of Italian maiolica at the time of the Renaissance. It had its own distinctive style and produced some of the most beautiful yellow lustreware which at the time was innovative and unparalleled. The Grazia factory dates back to the early 1500s and has remained within the family right up to the present day. Today there are 30 employees. The factory itself is a wonderful old building where all the name and room signs and many of the architectural details are in maiolica tiles. Today, under the direction of Dr Ubaldo Grazia, it is a thriving and highly organised business, and exports approximately 80% of its products to the USA.

Using a local red clay, the majority of pots are thrown; the rest press-moulded or jiggered and jolleyed. The bisque firing is to 1050°C, the glost 920°C. In deference to the large American clientele, the glaze is lead-free, but still opacified with tin. Decoration is all handpainted and uses the

Modern tableware with traditional (Renaissance) ornament. Grazia factory, Deruta.

pouncing technique for reproduction of designs. A transparent overglaze, similar to the *coperta*, is sprayed on over the painted surface to brighten and intensify the colours. Lustreware is still made, fired in a wood kiln. Other wares are fired in gas and electric kilns.

Grazia's stated aim is 'to be faithful to the old forms and to the old character of the tradition and at the same time to adapt to modern taste'. Grazia's production falls roughly into three categories: one is devoted to the reproduction of historical models. These copies are executed with such fidelity, precision and skill that they can hardly be accused of pastiche. As well as these exercises in pure historicism, there are more hybrid pieces which combine traditional Deruta ornamentation with modern tableware forms (there was no such thing as maiolica tableware in the 16th century). Grazia has also sought to update its image and broaden the range of wares by inviting contemporary artists from Italy and all over the world to design tableware and other pieces.

The historical copies and traditionally-inspired pieces made by Grazia form the mainstay of his business. They are exported in quantity and are a testimony to their great desirability for a large clientele. Their attraction seems to lie in their representation of a generally accepted idea of beauty. Their very resonance of antiquity, evocative of a golden age, is seen as proof of the owner's indisputable taste. They are a safe choice, involving no aesthetic risks on the part of

Reproduction of 16th-century drug jar by the Grazia factory, Deruta.

Pippin Drysdale, plate made at the Grazia factory, 1991.
Drysdale was given the freedom to develop colourful patterns that could be copied without much difficulty. All new designs are photographed, catalogued, and prototypes are displayed for potential purchasers. Of her time spent at Grazia, Drysdale says, . . . It helped me to resolve the problems of where to put a design, how to paint it, what works or doesn't. It was a constant challenge to find the feeling of painting with such bright colours onto the unctuous white maiolica glaze, which inspired much freer and more open designs, often depicting Australian symbols . . .' (see pp. 75 and 155 for examples of her recent studio work).

the purchaser. They also endow the owner with a certain status, for they are expensive, luxury hand-made items associated in people's minds with tangible symbols of power. Anne Lajoix [2] puts forward another reason for this phenomenon – the perception of the present as inferior to the past. These historical reproductions are reassuring reminders of the 'good old days'. Imitation has always been an integral component of the tin-glaze tradition although aesthetic conventions were formerly much more circumscribed; pedagogy and practice in the fine arts totally validated the practice of historicism and placed more emphasis on technique than on originality. Nonetheless, there is no such thing as an objective copy; the context of a different cultural climate – new materials, tastes and techniques – will inevitably give rise to both modifications on the part of the maker and altered perceptions on the part of the observer.

A HOPEFUL DIALOGUE:

Marc Camille Chaimowicz
at Nevers and Quimper

In 1988, at the instigation of the Direction Régionale d'Art Contemporain of Burgundy, artist Marc Camille Chaimowicz was invited to work in collaboration with François Bernard at his Fayencerie d'Art in Nevers to design a new range of products.

François Bernard's Fayencerie is one of the three active family workshops in Nevers. It is not a large concern – there are 12 workers altogether – but it is a thriving one, its reputation built on the reproduction of models from the 16th–18th centuries. These objects are considered highly collectable. Techniques remain traditional: the body is a blend of lime marl and local red clay; the bisque firing is to 1000°C, the glost 960°C; the glaze is lead-based and opacified with tin; most pots are thrown and designs are hand-painted with the assistance of pouncing.

Reproduction of a 16th century Nevers ewer, ht 38cm, by Fayencerie d'Art Bernard, Nevers.

Marc Camille Chaimowicz, group of work designed for Fayencerie d'Art Bernard, 1990. The large vase is 38 cm tall.

The only concession to modern technology is the use of slip-casting for certain shapes and electric kilns for firing. And yet, in inviting Chaimowicz to design for them, François Bernard has shown his openness to innovative reassessments of a traditional craft.

And so, over a period of 18 months, Chaimowicz made a total of 10 visits to the Fayencerie. During the course of these visits he came to establish a working dialogue with Bernard and his technicians, got to know the materials and techniques and what they could achieve for him.[3] Chaimowicz has completely bypassed the traditional pictorial approach to tin glaze, working instead from a more Modernist concern with growth and structure. He became very interested in the tactility of the materials and has exploited this aspect in his use both of relief and unglazed areas. The tin glaze is used either on its own or in combination with coloured textured mottling. His overall intention was to design pottery for mass-production which would be both accessible and affordable

to the general public. The five designs of Chaimowicz are now part of the regular Bernard production (constituting about 5% of the total output), and are sold in Bernard's own retail outlet as well as being marketed at the Nevers Biennales. Through this successful initiative, Bernard's professional status has been enhanced and he is regarded by others as an enterprising and innovative faiencier. It is encouraging that his example is now being followed in similar establishments.

Marc Camille Chaimowicz, Bonbonnières (sweet jars) 'Nic Nac', Fayencerie d'Art Bernard, Nevers.

Having learned much from his experience at Nevers, Chaimowicz went on to participate in several projects with the H.B. Henriot faienceries at Quimper. Production of faience at Quimper began in the late 17th century, when it was an offshoot of Rouen. The Henriot factory was established in the 19th century. The famous genre decoration of Breton figures, which has become a trademark of Quimper, was introduced by Alfred Beau, artist and director of Henriot, in the 1870s. The factory remained in the family up until 1984 when it was bought over by Paul Janssens, an American importer. It now employs a workforce of over 100 and is enjoying renewed prosperity. In the USA recently, Quimper was voted the most collectable type of pottery. The Henriot faienceries have a history of collaboration with artists and were particularly innovative in their stoneware designs of the

Marc Camille Chaimowicz, working drawings for the Nevers project 1988–90.

1920s and 1930s (Odetta series). In the spirit of his predecessors, the present managing director, Paul Marest, is aware of the importance of investing in the contemporary and is prepared to take some chances in this area.

Chaimowicz is currently involved with H.B. Henriot on two projects: one, architectural, is the design of a ceramic tile frieze which will be incorporated in the new railway station at Quimper; the other, domestic, is the design of a coffee service for production. The architectural project is a sequel to the successful completion of a tile frieze for the College de Pacé, near Rennes. They represent Chaimowicz's first attempts to translate drawn motifs on to a ceramic surface and relate closely to his fine art work. The coffee service too is a kind of three-dimensional progression from his recent paintings.

Factories have been surprised at the degree of Chaimowicz's active commitment to the projects. To provide a well-thought out three-dimensional maquette for the coffee pot was unusual – 'normally we just get a drawing', he was told! The aspect that has been the most problematic has been the translation of the colours and again, Chaimowicz has made sure he was closely involved with all stages of research. For Chaimowicz the art of design lies in the ability to 'appropriate other people's significant skills' although this partnership can also be reduced to a 'confrontation of differences' and be frustrating in its long-drawn-out time base. The fact that the designer is not a hands-on person can aggravate the confrontation, but it also has a positive side; not tied to materials, the naive eye of the non-potter can see them in an entirely fresh way – a good example of this freshness can be seen in Chaimowicz's unconventional use of unglazed areas in his work for Nevers.

Chaimowicz has an integrated approach to his work in the fine and applied arts. His ceramic designs are closely related to his pictorial ideas. His painting has the lightness of a Dufy or a Matisse and yet is, in his own words, 'oblique and understated'. Even when working in a more formal way at Nevers, the contours and punctuating relief details are echoes of the leitmotifs which permeate his work. He does feel however that there is a distinction between the two activities, not of hierarchy, more of modus operandi

Teapot by the Henriot faiencerie, Quimper, 19th century.
Oriental-inspired dragon spout and handle in chrome green contrast with the typical Quimper folk decoration of Breton figures.
Collection Anne Barlow. Photograph by Douglas Cape.

Statuette of Saint Anne, the Henriot faiencerie, Quimper, 1930s.
Religious faience statuettes such as this would have had their place in every Breton house. Their manufacture at Quimper dates back to the 18th century.
Collection Anne Barlow. Photograph by Douglas Cape.

Marc Camille Chaimowicz, sketch for coffee pot, 1991, for production at H.B. Henriot, Quimper.

Marc Camille Chaimowicz, 'Sept 89', charcoal and pastel, 24 cm x 35 cm.

Marc Camille Chaimowicz, designs for frieze of tiles at the College de Pacé, Rennes, made by H.B. Henriot, Quimper, 1991.

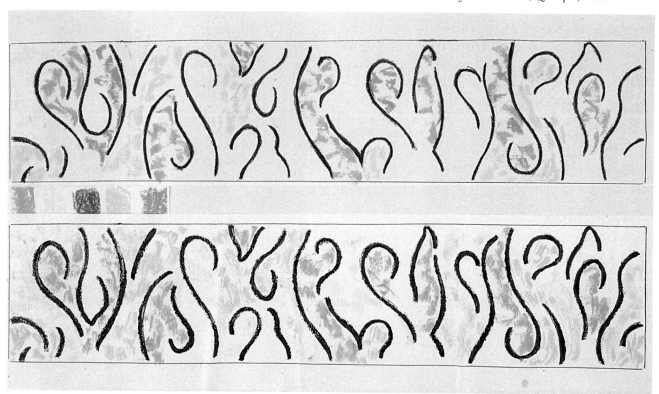

and relationship; in designing for the applied arts, there is a shift of emphasis from the subjective to the objective, from the intimate to the anonymous, from the singular to the plural, from the speculative and the unfinished to the concrete and the complete.

'Design gives us answers, Fine Art poses questions. We take meaning from Design . . . and give meaning to Fine Art.'[4]

Minerva Project
Tichelaars Royal Makkum Ceramics and Tile Manufactory dates back to the 17th century. Today, a workforce of 100 continues production of traditional designs. Pots are jiggered, jolleyed, moulded and slip-cast, in a local lime-bearing clay. The glaze is lead-based and opacified with tin; designs are hand-painted with the aid of *sponsen* (pouncing). 500,000 tiles are made each year, all hand-rolled into a wooden frame. In addition to maintaining the traditional range of designs, Tichelaars have also been open to a variety of collaborative projects with Dutch artists. The Minerva in Makkum 1990 was one such project and involved graduates of the Minerva art academy in Groningen in the creation of contemporary designs for existing Makkum forms.

Notes
[1] Artigas, J.L and Corredor-Matheos, J, *Spanish Folk Ceramics of Today*, Barcelona (Editorial Blume, 1970)
[2] Anne Lajoix, 'Céramique et mise en abîme de l'imitation', in *Caravelles 2*, catalogue of the 2e Quadriennale Internationale de Design, Lyon 1991
[3] Examples of all the various stages of research have now been preserved at the Musée de Cosne and constitute a useful educational tool for students.
[4] *Beaux Arts et Arts Appliqués*, Marc Camille Chaimowicz (Musée de Cosne, France, The Showroom, London)

Other sources of reference for this chapter:

Besacier, Hubert, 'Des créateurs face à la tradition', also in *Caravelles 2* (see above)
Carretero, A. et al., *Ceramica Popular de Andalucia*, Madrid (Edicion Nacional)
Fontenla, Renata, 'Some Spanish Potteries', *Ceramic Review*, no.74, 1982
Koblitz, Karen, 'A Love Affair with Italy', *Ceramics: Art and Perception*, no. 6, 1991

Grytsje de Jong, untitled, diam. 38.5, made at Tichelaars, Makkum (Minerva in Makkum project, 1990).

Traditional Makkum pattern for this plate.

FERRO LEADLESS GLAZE FRITS – EMPIRICAL FORMULAS (Mols)

Frit No.	Mol. Wt.	K_2O	Na_2O	Li_2O	CaO	MgO	BaO	SrO	ZnO	Al_2O_3	B_2O_3	S_1O_2	F	ZrO_2	Fusion Temp °C
3110	260.6	.064	.643	–	.293	–	–	–	–	.094	.098	3.03			765
3124	278.1	.020	.282	–	.698	–	–	–	–	.270	.550	2.56			875
3134	190.5	–	.316	–	.684	–	–	–	–	–	.632	1.47			790
3185	807.2	–	1.00	–	–	–	–	–	–	–	4.43	7.27			735
3195		–	.330	–	.670	–	–	–	–	.390	1.20	2.60			790
3211	133.4	–	–	–	1.00	–	–	–	–	–	1.11	–			950
3240	207.6	.012	.152	–	.326	–	.107	–	.403	.018	.295	1.36	.209	.172	820
3269	354.5	.306	.641	–	.009	–	–	–	.044	.462	.778	2.95	.300		765
3278	270.6	–	.669	–	.331	–	–	–	–	–	.842	2.53			765
3292	287.3	.095	.141	.042	.535	.055	–	.132	–	.301	.235	2.92			790
5301	247.2	.134	.765	–	.101	–	–	–	–	.274	.418	1.72	1.12		820
6649	Proprietory Frit – high zirconium content – use for matte crackle at low temperatures
6650	Comments as above

POTTERYCRAFTS FRITS

FRITS	PRODUCT NUMBER	BASES						AMPHOTERIC		ACID		MOLE- CULAR WEIGHT	FIRING RANGE
		PbO	Na_2O	K_2O	CaO	Li_2O	ZnO	MgO	Al_2O_3	SiO_2	B_2O_3		
Lead Bisilicate	P2950	1.00	–	–	–	–	–	–	0.086	1.86	–	343.5	900–1100°C
Lead Sesquisilicate	P2951	1.00	–	–	–	–	–	–	TiO_2 0.125 –	1.54	–	325.4	880–1080°C
Lead Borosilicate	P2952	0.45	0.066	0.019	0.415	0.050	–	–	0.288	5.2	1.2	543.9	900–1100°C
Borax Frit	P2953	–	0.369	0.074	0.556	–	–	–	0.506	1.955	0.848	230.27	900–1100°C
Borax Frit	P2955	–	0.417	0.214	0.366	–	–	0.002	1.205	1.884	0.425	234.7	920–1050°C
Borax Frit	P2957	–	0.264	0.132	0.594	–	–	0.010	0.418	4.703	0.963	454.2	1000–1100°C
Borax Frit	P2958	–	0.515	0.057	0.428	–	–	–	0.523	4.31	1.06	448.69	920–1100°C
High Temp Borax Frit	P2959	–	0.4	–	0.3	–	0.05	0.25	0.3	5.	1.	469.7	1030–1180°C
Soft Borax Frit	P2964	–	1.00	–	–	–	–	–	–	3.074	2.54	425.2	750–1000°C
Standard Alkaline Frit	P2961	–	0.49	–	0.509	–	–	–	0.806	2.599	0.911	361.5	900–1100°C
High Alkaline Frit	P2962	BaO 0.105 –	0.58	0.21	0.105	–	–	–	0.093	1.660	0.105	193.6	880–1060°C
Soft Alkaline Frit	P2963		0.633	0.293	0.067	–	–	0.006	0.783	2.313	0.876	351.4	750–1000°C
Low Expansion Frit	P2960	Formula not available											1020–1150°C
White Opaque Zircon Frit	P2956	–	0.39	–	0.5	–	0.11	–	0.165	3.5	ZrO_2 0.3 0.815	390.	940–1150°C
Calcium Borate Frit	P2954	–	–	–	1.00	–	–	–	0.097	0.609	1.5	207.1	1050–1160°C

ORTON PYROMETRIC CONES

(The Edward Orton Jr Ceramic Foundation, Westerville, Ohio)

Small cones; squatting temperatures when heated at:			Small cones; squatting temperatures when heated at:			Small cones; squatting temperatures when heated at:		
Cone no.	300°C/hr	540°F/hr	Cone no.	300°C/hr	540°F/hr	Cone no.	300°C/hr	540°F/hr
022	630*	1165*	010	919	1686	3	1196	2185
021	643	1189	09	955	1751	4	1209	2208
020	666	1231	08	983	1801	5	1221	2230
019	723	1333	07	1008	1846	6	1255	2291
018	752	1386	06	1023	1873	7	1264	2307
017	784	1443	05	1062	1944	8	1300	2372
016	825	1517	04	1098	2008	9	1317	2403
015	843	1549	03	1131	2068	10	1330	2426
014	870*	1596*	02	1148	2098	11	1336	2437
013	880*	1615*	01	1178	2152	12	1355	2471
012	900*	1650*	1	1179	2154			
011	915*	1680*	2	1179	2154			

Large cones; squatting temperatures when heated at:				Large cones; squatting temperatures when heated at:			
Cone no.	60°C/hr	108°F/hr	150°C/hr	270°F/hr	Cone no.	60°C/hr	108°F/hr	150°C/hr	270°F/hr
022	576*	1069*	586*	1086*	04	1050	1922	1060	1940
021	602	1116	614	1137	03	1086	1987	1101	2014
020	625	1157	635	1175	02	1101	2014	1120	2048
019	668	1234	683	1261	01	1117	2043	1137	2079
018	696	1285	717	1323	1	1136	2077	1154	2109
017	727	1341	747	1377	2	1142	2088	1162	2124
016	764	1407	792	1458	3	1152	2106	1168	2134
015	790	1454	804	1479	4	1168	2134	1186	2167
014	834	1533	838	1540	5	1177	2151	1196	2185
013	836*	1537*	861*	1582*	6	1201	2194	1222	2232
012	856*	1573*	872*	1602*	7	1215	2219	1240	2264
011	872*	1602*	883*	1621*	8	1236	2257	1263	2305
010	880*	1616*	890*	1634*	9	1260	2300	1280	2336
09	915	1679	923	1693	10	1285	2345	1305	2381
08	945	1733	955	1751	11	1294	2361	1315	2399
07	973	1783	984	1803	12	1306	2383	1326	2419
06	991	1816	999	1830	13	1321	2410	1346	2455
05	1031	1888	1046	1915	14	1388	2530	1366	2491

[1] The temperature equivalents shown for small cones may be used as a guideline for determining deformation temperatures of Orton pyrometric bars. However, Orton pyrometric bars were intended solely for use in automatic shut-off devices. They are not to be mounted in plaques or pats and used on a kiln shelf. Orton pyrometric bars were designed to deform in a shut-off when an Orton self-supporting cone of the same number is properly deformed on the kiln shelf.

[2] These temperatures are approximate. They were not determined at the National Bureau of Standards.

[1] The temperature equivalents shown for the large cones may be used as a guideline for determining deformation temperatures of self-supporting cones. However the self-supporting cones may deform at approximately 2°C higher than the large cones depending on the mounting height of the large cones.

[2] These temperatures are approximate. They were not determined at the National Bureau of Standards.

List of suppliers

This list is not intended to be comprehensive and relates chiefly to the products mentioned in the foregoing text.

UK

Ceramatech Ltd
Unit 16
Frontier Works
33 Queen Street
London N17 8JA
Tel: 081 885 4492
(*colours and general supplies*)

Potterycrafts Ltd
Campbell Road
Stoke on Trent ST4 4ET
Tel: 0782 272 444
(*colours and general supplies*)

Deancraft Fahey
12 Spedding Road
Fenton Industrial Estate
Stoke on Trent ST4 2ST
Tel: 0782 414400
(*colours and general supplies*)

A. S. Handover Ltd
Angel Yard
Highgate High Street
London N6 5JU
Tel: 081 340 0665
(*brushes*)

Valentines Clay Products
Birches Head Road
Hanley
Stoke-on-Trent
Tel: 0782 271200
(*clays*)

Potclays Ltd
Brickkiln Lane
Etruria
Stoke on Trent ST4 7BP
Tel: 0782 219816
(*clays and general supplies*)

Brannams
Roundswell Industrial Estate
Barnstaple
Devon
Tel: 0271 43035
(*Fremington clay*)

USA

Ferro Frit Corporation
4150 East 56th Street
PO Box 6550
Cleveland
Ohio 4410
Tel: (216) 641 8580
(*frits*)

Cedar Heights Clay Company
PO Box 295
Oak Hill, Ohio
Tel: (614) 682 7794
(*Redart and other clays*)

Mason Color Works Inc
PO Box 76
East Liverpool
Ohio 43920
(*stains*)

Columbus Clay
1049 W Fifth Ave
Columbus
OH 43212
Tel: (614) 294 1114
(*have odd lots of industrial stains including O'Hommel, Pemco, Johnson Matthey, Ferro etc. Request their non-Mason stain information sheet*)

Standard Ceramics
PO Box 4435
Pittsburgh
PA 15205
Tel: (412) 276 6333
(*stains*)

A.P. Green Industries Inc
Green Boulevard
Mexico
Missouri 65265
Tel: (314) 473 3626
(*fireclay*)

The Feldspar Corporation
PO Box 8
Edgar, Florida
Tel: (904) 481 2421
(*EPK – Edgar Plastic Kaolin*)

H.C. Muddox Company
4875 Bradshaw Road
Sacramento
California 95827
(*grog*)

Kentucky-Tennessee Clay Company
PO Box 6002
Mayfield
KY 42066
(*Old Mine #4 ball clay*)

International Minerals and Chemical Corporation
Consolidated Feldspar Dept
Old Orchard Road
Stokie
Illinois 60078
(*Kona F-4 and other felspars*)

Leslie's Ceramics
1212 San Pablo Ave
Berkely
California 94706
Tel: (510) 524 7363
(*stains*)

General Colour and Chemical Co
PO Box 7
Minerva
Ohio 44657
Tel: (216) 868 4161
(*stains*)

O'Hommel Co
Hope and Maple Streets
Carnegie
Pennsylvania 15106
(*stains*)

A.R.T. Studio Clay Co
1555 Lovis Ave
Elk Grove Village
Illinois 60007
Tel: (708) 593 6060
(*V-Gum-T and general supplies*)

Seattle Pottery Supply
35 South Hanford, Seattle
Washington 98134
Tel: (206) 587 0570
(*general*)

List of museums

The following listing has been compiled as a guide to some of the museums in Europe and the USA, which to my knowledge, or on recommendation, possess important or interesting collections of tin glaze. It should not be considered in any sense a complete or definitive directory.

UK

Victoria and Albert Museum
London
(*most comprehensive*)

British Museum
London
(*Islamic, Hispano-Moresque, Italian, German, English*)

Wallace Collection
London
(*Hispano-Moresque, Italian*)

Museum of London
London

Courtauld Institute Galleries
London University
(*small but choice collection*)

Ashmolean Museum
Oxford
(*Islamic, Italian, English*)

Fitzwilliam Museum
Cambridge
(*Glaisher Collection: English, Italian, Dutch, Spanish, German, Swiss*)

Saffron Walden Museum, Essex
(*English, Dutch*)

Bristol City Art Gallery

Royal Museum of Scotland
Edinburgh

City Museums of:
Stoke-on-Trent
Manchester
Glasgow

USA

J.Paul Getty Museum,
Malibu, California
(*Italian*)

Freer Gallery of Art
Washington DC
(*Islamic*)

Museum of the Hispanic Society of America,
New York
(*Hispano-Moresque*)

Metropolitan Museum of Art
New York
(*comprehensive, also has Robert Lehman collection of Italian maiolica*)

CANADA

George R.Gardiner Museum
Toronto

FRANCE

Musée Nationale de Céramique,
Sevres
(*comprehensive*)

Musée de Cluny
Paris

Musée des Beaux Arts
Quimper

Musée Municipal
Nevers

Musée des Arts Decoratifs
Strasbourg

Musée des Beaux Arts et de la Ceramique
Rouen

Musée Cantini
Marseilles

Musée des Beaux Arts
Musée des Arts Decoratifs
Lyons

ITALY

Museo Internazionale delle Ceramiche
Faenza
(*comprehensive*)

Museo Nazionale del Bargello
Florence

Museo Civico Medievale
Bologna

Museo del Vino
Torgiano (nr Deruta)
(*Pottery associated with wine-making and drinking*)

Museo Civico
Pesaro

NETHERLANDS

Rijksmuseum, Amsterdam
(*Italian, Dutch*)

Museum Het Princesshof
(Nederlands Keramiek Museum)
Leeuwarden

Museum Boymans-van Beuningen,
Rotterdam
(*Italian, Dutch*)

Gemeentemuseum
The Hague

SPAIN

Museo de Ceramica
Palau de Pedralbes
Barcelona

Museo Historica
Valencia

Museo Arqueologico
Madrid

Instituto 'Valencia de Don Juan'
Madrid

Bibliography

Books

Allan, J.W., *Islamic Ceramics*, Oxford (Ashmolean Museum, 1991)

Allan, J.W., *Medieval Middle Eastern Pottery*, Oxford, (Ashmolean Museum, 1971)

Altorfer Max (ed), *Margrit Linck*, Bern (Benteli Verlag, 1981)

Artigas J.L. and J. Correodor-Matheos, *Spanish Folk Ceramics of Today*, Barcelona, 1970 (Ed. Blume)

Berendsen, Anne, *Tiles, A General History*, London (Faber and Faber, 1967)

Fausto, Berti, *The Montelupo Ceramics*, London (Electa)

Britton, Frank, *London Delftware*, London (Jonathan Horne, 1987)

Britton, Frank, *English Delftware in the Bristol Collection*, London (Sotheby Publications, 1982)

Caiger-Smith, Alan, *Tin-glaze Pottery in Europe and the Islamic World*, London (Faber and Faber, 1973)

Caiger-Smith, Alan, *Lustre Pottery*, London (Faber and Faber, 1985); now also in paperback (Herbert Press)

Cameron, Elisabeth, *Encyclopaedia of Pottery and Porcelain – The Nineteenth and Twentieth Centuries*, London (Faber and Faber, 1986)

Carretero, A. et al., *Ceramica Popular de Andalucia*, Madrid (Editora Nacional, 1984)

Chaimowicz, Marc Camille, *Beaux Arts et Arts Appliqués* (Musée de Cosne, France and The Showroom, London, 1989)

Charleston, Robert (ed), *World Ceramics*, London (Hamlyn, 1968)

Charleston R.J., and D.F. Lunsingh Scheurleer, *English and Dutch Ceramics*, Tokyo (Kodansha – Masterpieces of Western Ceramic Art series, 1978)

Cooper, Emmanuel, *History of World Pottery*, London (Batsford, 1981)

Crafts Council Gallery, *The Omega Workshops 1913–19*, London, 1984 – exhibition catalogue; good essay by Fiona Macarthy on 'Roger Fry and the Omega Idea'

de Jonghe, Constance, *Delft Ceramics*, London (Pall Mall Press, 1970)

Dormer, Peter, *The New Ceramics Trends and Traditions* London (Thames and Hudson, 1986)

Drey, Rudolf, *Apothecary Jars*, London (Faber and Faber, 1978)

Fiocco, C. and G. Gherardi, *Ceramiche Umbre dal Medioevo allo Storicismo*, 2 vols. Faenza (Museo Internazionale delle Ceramiche, 1988)

Fourest, H.-P., *Delftware*, London (Thames and Hudson, 1980)

Fourest, H.-P., *French Ceramics*, Tokyo (Kodansha – Masterpieces of Western Ceramic Art series, 1978)

Frégnac, Claude, *La Faïence Européenne*, Fribourg (Office du Livre, 1976). Categorisation by style (e.g. Italianate, Classical, Rococo etc.)

Frothingham, Alice, *Lustreware of Spain*, New York (Hispanic Society of America, 1951)

Garner, F.H. and Michael Archer, *English Delftware*, London (Faber and Faber, 1972)

Giacomotti, J., *Faïences Françaises*, Fribourg (Office du Livre, 1963)

Grand Palais des Champs Elysees, Paris, *Faïences Françaises XVI-XVIII siecle*, 1980 – exhibition catalogue

Grube, Ernst J., *Islamic Pottery of the Eighth to the Fifteenth Century in the Keir Collection*, London (Faber and Faber, 1976)

Hayward Gallery, *The Arts of Islam*, The Arts Council of Great Britain, 1976 – exhibition catalogue

Hess, C., *J. Paul Getty Museum, Italian Maiolica of the Collections*, Malibu, 1988

Houston John and David Cripps, *Lucie Rie*, London (Craft Council, 1981)

Houston, John, *Craft Classics since the 1940s*, London, (Crafts Council, 1988)

Kallir, Jane, *Viennese Design and the Wiener Werkstätte*, New York (G. Brazillier in association with Galerie St Etienne, 1986)

Krisztinkovich, Bela, *Haban Pottery*, Budapest (Corvina Press, 1962)

Lajoix, Anne, *La Céramique en France 1925–47*, Paris (Sous le Vent, 1983)

Lane, Arthur, *Early Islamic Pottery*, London (Faber and Faber, 1947)

Lane, Arthur, *French Faience*, London (Faber and Faber, 1948)

Leach, Bernard, *A Potter's Book*, London (Faber and Faber, 1940)

Leach, Bernard, *The Potter's Challenge*, London (Souvenir Press, 1976)

Lipski L.L., and Michael Archer, *Dated English Delftware*, London (Sothebys, 1984)

Liverani, G., *Five Centuries of Italian Majolica*, New York (McGraw-Hill, 1960)

Musée des Arts Décoratifs, Paris, *Céramique Française Contemporaine* (exhibition catalogue) 1981

Musée des Beaux Arts, Quimper, *Quimper: Trois Siècles de Faience 1690–1990*, vol.1 illustrated history of Quimper production; vol.2 exhibition catalogue (black and white illus) (Editions Ouest-France – Ville de Quimper, 1990)

Nicola Jacobs Gallery, London, *Original Ceramics by Picasso*, exhibition catalogue, 1984

Palvarini and Casali, *La Ceramica a Mantova*, Ferrara (Belriguardo, 1987)

Pevsner, Nikolaus, *Pioneers of Modern Design*, London (Penguin, 1960)

Piccolpasso, Cipriano, *The Three Books of the Potter's Art* (1548), ed. by R. Lightbown and Alan Caiger-Smith, London (Scolar Press, 1978)

Pinkham, Roger, *Catalogue of Pottery by William De Morgan*, London (Victoria and Albert Museum – HMSO, 1973)

Pope-Hennessy, Sir John, *Luca Della Robbia*, Oxford (Phaidon, 1980)

Préaud, Tamara, and Serge Gauthier, *Ceramics of the 20th Century*, Oxford (Phaidon/Christies, 1982)

Rackham, Bernard, *Catalogue of the Glaisher Collection of Pottery and Porcelain in the Fitzwilliam Museum, Cambridge*, vols 1 and 2 (Antique Collectors Club, 1987)

Rackham, Bernard, *Early Netherlands Maiolica*, London (Geoffrey Bles, 1926)

Rackham, Bernard, *Italian Majolica*, London (Faber and Faber, 1965)

Rackham, Bernard, *Victoria and Albert Museum, Catalogue of Italian Maiolica*, vol 1 (Text) and vol 2 (Photographs), London (HMSO, 1977)

Ramié, Georges, *Ceramics of Picasso*, Barcelona (Ed. Poligrafa, 1985)

Rasmussen, J., *The Robert Lehman Collection* (Italian Maiolica), New York (Metropolitan Museum, 1989)

Ray, Anthony, *English Delftware Pottery in the Robert Hall Warren Collection*, London (Faber and Faber, 1968)

Rawson, Philip, *Ceramics*, London (Oxford University Press, 1971)

Schnyder, R., *Winterthurer Keramik*, Zurich (Schweizerisches Landesmuseum) and Winterthur (Museum Lindengut, 1989 – exhibition catalogue)

Schweiger, Werner, *Wiener Werkstätte: Design in Vienna 1903–1932*, London (Thames and Hudson, 1984)

Shearman, John, *Mannerism*, London (Penguin, 1990)

Stoke on Trent City Museum and Art Gallery, *Alan Caiger-Smith*, exhibition catalogue, 1984

Van Dam, J.D., *Nederlandse Tegels*, Utrecht/Antwerp (Veen/Reflex)

Vydra, Josef, and Ludvik Kunz, *Painting on Folk Ceramics*, London (Spring Books) – no date of publication, probably 1960s.

Watson, Oliver, *British Studio Pottery – The Victoria and Albert Museum Collection*, Oxford (Phaidon-Christies, 1990)

Watson, W., *Italian Renaissance Maiolica from the William A. Clark Collection* (Scala, 1986)

Wechsler, Susan, *Low Fire Ceramics – A New Direction in American Clay*, New York (Watson-Guptill, 1981).

Wilson, Timothy, *Ceramic Art of the Italian Renaissance*, London (British Museum Publications, 1987 – exhibition catalogue)

Wilson, Timothy, *Maiolica – Italian Renaissance Ceramics in the Ashmolean Museum*, Oxford (Ashmolean Museum, 1989)

Articles

Besacier, Hubert, 'Des créateurs face à la tradition' and Anne Lajoix, 'Céramique et mise en abîme de l'imitation', both in *Caravelles 2*, catalogue of the 2e Quadriennale Internationale de Design, Lyon 1991.

Britton, Alison, 'Sevres with Krazy Kat', *Crafts Magazine*, no.61, 1983.

Caiger-Smith, Alan, 'Why Decorate Pots?', *Crafts Magazine*, no.52, 1981.

Cochrane, Bruce, 'Expressive, Utilitarian Earthenware', *Ceramics Monthly*, Nov. 1990.

Collins, Judith, 'Roger Fry and Omega Pottery', *Ceramic Review*, no.86, 1984.

Espagnet, Françoise, 'André Metthey et les Fauves: la renaissance de la faïence au début du XX siècle', *Revue de la Céramique et du Verre*, no.19, 1984.

Gaimster, David et al., 'The Continental stove tile fragments from St Mary Graces, London in their British and European context,' *Post-Medieval Archaeology*, vol. 24, 1990

Girard, Sylvie, 'Gilbert Portanier', *Revue de la Céramique et du Verre*, no.19, 1984.

Harrod, Tanya, 'The Forgotten Fifties', *Crafts Magazine*, no.100, 1989.

'In the Beginning was Earthenware', *Studio Potter*, vol.11, no.2 (articles by Stanley Mace Anderson, Walter Ostrom and Andrea Gill)

Ostermann, Matthias, 'From Pots to Art: Out of the Kitchen and into the Living Room', *Ceramic Review*, no.123, 1990.

Woodman, George, 'Ceramic Decoration and the Concept of Ceramics as a Decorative Art', *American Ceramics*, vol.I, no.1, Winter 1982.

Technical

Fraser, Harry, *Ceramic Faults and their Remedies*, London (A & C Black, 1986)

Hamer, Frank and Janet Hamer, *The Potter's Dictionary of Materials and Techniques*, 2nd edn, London (A & C Black, 1986)

Parmelee, C.W, *Ceramic Glazes*, Chicago, 1951

Shaw, Kenneth, *Ceramic Colours and Pottery Decoration*, London (Faber and Faber, 1962)

Main historical centres of manufacture of tin-glazed earthenware in Europe

1 Talavera de la Reina	23 Pesaro	45 Strasbourg	66 Glasgow
2 Seville	24 Urbino (Castel Durante)	46 Lunéville	67 Dublin
3 Triana	25 Gubbio	47 Niderviller	68 Belfast
4 Valencia (Manises)	26 Deruta	48 Quimper	69 Winterthur
5 Paterna	27 Rome	49 St Amand-les-Eaux	70 Hamburg
6 Teruel	28 Naples	50 Lille	71 Berlin
7 Malaga	29 Castelli	51 St Omer	72 Augsburg
8 Puente del Arzobispo	30 Padua	52 Sinceny	73 Nuremberg
9 Alcora	31 Turin	53 Sceaux	74 Ansbach
10 Reus	32 Lodi	54 Paris	75 Frankfurt-am-Main
11 Barcelona	33 Milan	55 Antwerp	76 Hanau
12 Granada	34 Albisola	56 Haarlem	77 Höchst
13 Murcia	35 Savona	57 Delft	78 Fulda
14 Lisbon	36 Palermo	58 Rotterdam	79 Dorotheenthal
15 Orvieto	37 Caltagirone	59 Makkum	80 Dresden
16 Florence	38 Rouen	60 Amsterdam	81 Holić
17 Siena	39 Nevers	61 Liverpool	82 Prague
18 Faenza	40 Lyons	62 London (Southwark, Lambeth)	83 Warsaw
19 Venice	41 Nîmes	63 Bristol (Brislington)	84 Budapest
20 Ravenna	42 Montpellier	64 Wincanton	85 Kiel
21 Cafaggiolo	43 Marseilles	65 Norwich	86 Stockelsdorf
22 Montelupo	44 Moustiers		

Index

INDEX
Numbers in italic indicate an illustration

Abaquesne, Masseot, of Rouen 37, *38*
Abbasid dynasty ware 12–15
Adam and Eve chargers 53
Alcora 60
Aldgate 51, 52
Andersen, Stanley Mace 144, *146*
Andreoli, Maestro Giorgio, of Gubbio *33*
Andries, Guido 44
  Jasper 51
antimony yellows 85
Anabaptist movement *see* Habaner ware
Antwerp 36, 44–5
Arbuckle, Linda *151*
archaic maiolica 24–5
artist-potter, notion of 65ff
Austria 36
Avelli, Francesco Xanto 30

Baroque art, influence of 37
Barwick, Gail *147*
Baudisch, Gudrun 66
Bauhaus 66
Bell, Vanessa 69
Bérain, Jean, court designer 41
Bernard, François, Fayencerie d'Art 163–4
berretino glaze 32, 79
bianco sopra bianco 32, 57, 79
bianchi di Faenza 33, *36*, 37, 63
Billington, Dora 71, 102
bleu de Nevers 38, 55, *56*
blue-dash chargers 52–3, *54*
Bohemia 36
Bologna 28
Bristol 51, 53, *55, 57, 59*
Britton, Alison 8, 73, 133
Bracquemond, Félix 66
Brébiette, Pierre *39*
Brou, France 37
brushes and brushwork 92–3

cadmium release *see* toxicity
Caiger-Smith, Alan 106–112 and passim
Calm-Wierink, Lotte 66
Cardew, Michael 8
Carnegy, Daphne *frontispiece, 99,* 133–6
  painting technique, 93–4
Castel Durante 30, *32, 36*
Castelli 38
Chaimowicz, Marc Camille 163–7
chargers 52–3, *54*
Chinese porcelain, influence of 7, 12, 38, 41, 42, 51, 55, 61
Chinoiserie, English 55, 57
chrome-tin pinks and reds 85
Clark, Ann 73, 74, *95*
Clark, Kenneth 73
clays, gault 52
  for tin glaze 77–8

Cochrane, Bruce 8, 136–8
colouring oxides for maiolica painting 82–5
cones, pyrometric, charts 169
Conrade brothers, of Albisola 37
contour panel device in decoration 14, *15, 26,* 28
cuerda seca technique 21, *23*

Daw, Deirdre *9,* 149, *150*
Deck, Théodore 66
decoration
  author's painting technique 93–4
  brushes and brushwork 92–3
  glaze on glaze 96
  on-glaze enamels 96, *99* (see also enamels)
  painting mediums 93
  slips 96, *99*
Delft and Delftware, Dutch 39, 45–50
Deruta 32, *33*
Dorigny, Michel 37, *39*
Dublin 51
Dufy, Raoul, and Artigas 69, *70*
Drysdale, Pippin *75, 155, 162*

Egypt, 13, 15–16
enamels on tin glaze 96
  French 41, *43*
  Minai 18–19
  see also Katzenstein, Lisa
Escallier, Eléanore 66

Faenza 26, 27, 28, *29*
faience, definitions 37ff
famiglia verde, la 25, *26*
Fatimid pottery 15–16
Favre family 70
Fayyum 16
Fazackerley ware 58
felspars, and secondary fluxes, in glazes 80
fine arts, influence of 25, *26,* 28, 30, 32, 37, 57 and passim
firing 97
Florence 25, 26
Floris family of Antwerp 44
flower painting, Dutch 45–6
fluxes, in glazes 79–80
Frijtom, Frederick van *47,* 48
frit-paste body 17
frits, use of in glazes 79–80
  formulae 168
Fritsch, Elizabeth 8, 73, 133
Fraser, Harry, on toxicity 98
Fry, Roger *see* Omega Workshops

Gallé, Emile 66
galleyware 51
Germany 42, *62, 63*
Gill, Andrea 8, 112–117
Glasgow 51
glaze, composition today 79–80
  historical 78–9
  preparation of 90
glaze faults 97–8

glazing 90–91
Grant, Duncan *67,* 69
Grazia factory Deruta 161–2
Gubbio 32–3
Gustin, Jane 9, *157–8*

Habaner ware 63–4
Hall, Morgen 140–2
Henriot, H B, faiencerie, Quimper 70, 164–6
Hispano-Moresque ware 19–23
Hine, Margaret 71, *73, 104*

imitation, phenomenon of 7–8
Islamic, early 12–19
Isnik ware, influence of 33, 53
istoriato maiolica 30–31 and passim
Italo-Moresque style 26–8

Jansen, Jacob of Antwerp 51
Japan, influence of 50, 66

Kashan 16–18
Katzenstein, Lisa 96, 98, *99*
Keyes, Phyllis *67,* 69, 73
kilns 88–9
Kovacs, Margrit 66

Lajoix, Anne 10, 162
Lambeth 51, *54, 55,* 57
Leach, Bernard 8, 22, *23*
lead release *see* toxicity
Léger, Fernand 70
Linck, Margrit 9, 129–32
Liverpool 51, 52, *58*
London 51ff
Lurçat, Jean 70, *71*
lustre (technique) 13, 86–8
  see also Alan Caiger-Smith, Alan Peascod, Sutton Taylor
lustreware, Abbasid 12–15
  Deruta 32, *33*
  Fatimid 15–16
  Gubbio 32–3
  Hispano-Moresque 19–21
  Persian 16–17
Lyons 37

maiolica, definitions 7, 24
  archaic (Orvieto) 24–5
  High Renaissance ornament 31, *32,* 36
  Italo-Moresque 26–9
  istoriato 30–31
  severe (Tuscan) 25–6
Majolica Works *147*
Malling jugs 51
Makkum 50, 167
Malaga 19
Manessi, Agalis 8, 139–140
Manises 19
Mannerism 31
Mantegna 30
Marseilles 37, 41, *43,* 60
Mayodon, Jean 70
Méheut, Mathurin 70
metal release in glazes 98–100

Metthey, André, and the Fauves 68
Mexico 64
Michelangelo *31*
Minai ware 18–19
Montelupo 33, *34*, *61*
Moravia 36
Morgan, William de 65–6
Morocco 64
Morris, William 65
Moustiers 37, *38*, 40–41, 60
museums, list of 171

Nel, Hylton *152*
Nevers 37, *39*
Newland, William 8, 71, 96, 102–105
Nîmes 37
Northern Dutch maiolica 45

'oak-leaf' ware 26
Obsieger, Robert 66
Omega Workshops 69
opacifiers 80–81
Orléans *41*
Orvieto ware 24–5
Ostermann, Matthias 9, 95, 121–4
Ostrom, Walter 8, 125–7

painting, mediums 93
  pigments 82–6
  technique, the author's 93–4
palette, Italian maiolica 28
Palmer, Jitka 9, 143
Paterna 19, 21, 25
peasant pottery in Spain and Italy
  159ff
Peascod, Alan 9, 87, 118–21
Peche, Dagobert 66
Picasso 8, 70–71
Piccolpasso, Cipriano 33, 76ff, 88, *95*
pigments 81–6
Pisano, Nicoluso of Triana 60

Poncelet, Jacqueline 8, 73
porcelain, influence of Chinese 12,
  37, 45
    German 41, 42
Portanier, Gilbert 9, 156
Portugal 61, 62
Poterat, Edmé of Rouen 40
Powolny, Michael 66
Puente del Arzobispo 60, *61*

Quatre Potiers, les 70

Raphael 8, 30, 31
Rawson, Philip on perspectival
  illusionism in Italian maiolica 31
Rayy 16–19
Reptile (Carlo Briscoe and Edward
  Dunn) *154*
Robbia, della, family and workshops
  28–9, *30*, 37
Rococo 41, 42
Rouen 39ff, 50
Royal portraits in English Delftware
  53, *54*
Rozman, Paul *148*

Savin, Maurice 69, *71*
Savino, Guido di 44
Selfridge, Carol and Richard 148, *151*
Seville 23, 60
Shackleton, Jason *150*
Shearman, John, on Mannerism 31
Siebert, Terry 145, *146*
Siena *27*
Singer, Susi 66
Simonovic, Ifigenia *95*
sintering 91–2
Slovakia 36
Southwark 51, *52*, *54*, 55, *56*
Strasbourg 40, 42
Switzerland 36

Sykes, Stephen 73
Symons, Ian 8, 153

tableware, French 39ff
Talavera 19, 45, 60
Taylor, Sutton 87
Teruel 21, *22*
Tichelaars factory of Makkum 50, 167
tiles, Dutch 45–6, *47*
    Kashan 17
    Portuguese 62
tin oxide 80–81 and passim
titanium dioxide 81
Toledo 60
Tower, James 71, *72*, 96
toxicity of materials and glazes 98–100
Triana 45, 60
Trianon de Porcelaine 39
tulip chargers 53, *54*

Urbino 30, *31*
    Nicola da 30

Valencia 19, *20*, *21*, 26
Venice 33, *35*, 38
Vergette, Nicholas 71, *72*
vernacular potteries of Spain and
  Italy 159–60
Vyne, The, Hampshire 44

wax resist 95
Wedgwood 7
whitewares, Dutch 48
    Faenza 33, *36*, 63
    later Italian 61
    London 55–6
Wiener Werkstätte 66
Wilhelm, Christian of Southwark 55
Winterthur 63
Woodman, George 9, 125, 136

Zirconium silicate 81